Shakespeare and Southern Writers
A Study in Influence

Philip C. Kolin
Editor

With a Foreword by
Lewis P. Simpson

UNIVERSITY PRESS OF MISSISSIPPI
Jackson

This book has been sponsored by the
University of Southern Mississippi

Library of Congress Cataloging in Publication Data
Main entry under title:

Shakespeare and southern writers.

Includes index.
1. American literature—Southern States—History and
criticism—Addresses, essays, lectures. 2. Shakespeare,
William, 1564–1616—Influence—Addresses, essays, lectures.
3. Southern States in literature—Addresses, essays,
lectures. 4. Influence (Literary, artistic, etc.)—Addresses, essays, lectures. I. Kolin, Philip C.
PS261.S4 1985   810'.9'975   85-5376
ISBN 0-87805-255-0

Contents

Acknowledgments

As with my earlier *Shakespeare in the South: Essays on Performance,* I want to thank the administration of the University of Southern Mississippi for sponsoring this volume. I am indebted to President Aubrey K. Lucas and Vice-Presidents Shelby F. Thames, Karen M. Yarbrough, and James H. Sims for their warm and continuing interest in my work. To Dr. John Edmond Gonzales, the Chairman of the University Press Committee, goes my special thanks; without his encouragement this project on Shakespeare and the South, which I envisioned long ago, would never have become a reality. My gratitude also goes to Seetha Srinivasan, the executive editor at the University Press, who diligently worked with me and the contributors to bring this and the preceding collection on Shakespeare in the South to publication. The contributors join me in thanking the various institutions and individuals that so generously allowed us to reprint the photographs of the authors who are the subject of this volume. Finally, I thank my wife, Janeen, and my two children, Eric and Kristin, who by the grace of God sustained me with their prayers and their love.

Philip C. Kolin

Foreword

Stacked neatly on a table in the parlor of the Grangerford home—a table handsomely ornamented with a "beautiful oil-cloth" cover that had "a red and blue spread-eagle painted on it, a painted border all around"—Huck Finn discovers several books. These include a family Bible, *Pilgrim's Progress* (filled with "statements" that "was interesting but tough"), and Dr. Gunn's *Family Medicine* ("which told you all about what to do if a body was sick or dead"). There was also a hymnal, a copy of Henry Clay's speeches, and a copy of *Friendship's Offering,* a nineteenth-century gift book, which was "full of beautiful stuff and poetry." Huck does not mention one book that would have been in the home of any literate antebellum family, including even one like the Grangerfords living out in the semifrontier South along the Mississippi River. That is, a volume of Shakespeare's plays. On his famous travels in America during the later eighteen-thirties and the early forties, Alexis de Tocqueville found "hardly a pioneer hut that does not contain a few odd volumes of Shakespeare." Recalling that he "read the feudal drama of *Henry V* for the first time in a log cabin," Tocqueville testifies to a fact of nineteenth-century American culture, the universal presence of Shakespeare. The Bible, John Bunyan's *Pilgrim's Progress,* Shakespeare's dramas: this trinity of secular-spiritual volumes was close to the heart of this culture. Nor does Mark Twain fail fully to recognize the Shakespearean ambience in Huck's world. The episode in *Huckleberry Finn* involving the Shakespearean performance by the river rascals, who masquerade as the Duke of Bridgewater and "the pore disappeared Dauphin, Looy the Seventeen, son of Looy the Sixteen and Marry Antonette," offers stronger testimony to the Shakespearean presence in the world along the Mississippi River than would a mere mention of his works on the Grangerford parlor table.

As Thomas J. Richardson demonstrates in his essay on Mark Twain and Shakespeare in this illuminating edition of essays by various scholars on the influence of Shakespeare on southern literature from William Gilmore Simms to Walker Percy, the author of *Huckleberry Finn* not only had an extensive reading knowledge of Shakespeare but knew his dramas as an intimate part of the cultural life that nurtured his own genius. Out of his vivid acquaintance with Shakespeare, Mark Twain constructed the parodic pastiche from *Hamlet, Macbeth,* and *Richard III* that the duke "calls back from recollection's vaults" as "Hamlet's Immortal Soliloquy." He "learns" the king to recite this ludicrous speech for the climax of the "Shakespearean Revival" he and the king undertake, in the guise of "David Garrick the younger" and "Edmund Kean the elder," in "a little one-horse town" located "pretty well down in the state of Arkansas." Presenting their show after an exciting circus performance in the afternoon, they draw only about twelve "Arkansas lunkheads," who, according to the duke, "couldn't come up to Shakespeare."

In one sense Mark Twain's burlesque of Shakespeare in *Huckleberry Finn* (and elsewhere) was prompted by a constant desire to deflate the pretentious, often false American valuation of Old World literature and art. But in a larger sense, as Richardson shows, Mark Twain's burlesque of Shakespeare is a deep-running comment on the quality of life that Huck sees, and explores, in his journey with Jim the slave down the great continental river. In his burlesquing of Shakespeare, to be sure, Mark Twain was moved by feelings like those that prompted Melville, when, in his celebration of Hawthorne in 1850, he decried the idolization of Shakespeare by Americans—so extreme, he says, that "You must believe in Shakespeare's unapproachability, or quit the country." Yet in making his satirical jibe at the American reverence for Shakespeare, Melville admitted that "few who extol" Shakespeare "have ever read him deeply," having perhaps no acquaintance with him save "on the tricky stage (which alone made, and is still making him his mere mob renown"). Those with a more intense understanding of Shakespeare, Melville observes, discern his essential greatness in his subtle search for meaning "in this world of lies," where "Truth is forced to fly like a scared white doe in the woodlands." She reveals herself only to "masters of the great Art of Telling the Truth," like Shakespeare, who understands that Truth can be seen only in "cunning glimpses," and told only "covertly and by snatches."

It is interesting to imagine what Thomas Jefferson might have made of *Adventures of Huckleberry Finn* if he had returned to earth and read the book when it appeared in 1885. Huck reports on the sorry condition of a country that the author of the Declaration of Independence had dreamed would be populated by a self-sufficient, educated citizenry living on their own free holds, freed forever from the corruption of Europe. But while Jefferson, we may suppose, would have found Mark Twain's story a confounding of his vision of the American redemption from European history, we may suppose too that he would have recognized Huck's account of life in the moral wasteland that was the southern frontier as a compelling representation of historical truth; for Jefferson, southern master and man of letters, no less than Melville and Mark Twain, understood the art of representing historical truth through fiction. In proposing a reading program to a young friend in 1771, Jefferson said: "I appeal to every reader of sentiment whether the fictitious murder of Duncan by Macbeth in Shakespeare does not excite in him as great a horror of villainy, as the real one of Henry IV, by Ravaillac as related by Davila? . . . Considering history as a moral exercise, her lessons would be too infrequent if confined to real life."

Living in his imagination the drama of the inception of the modern age—living the loss of the heroic, hierarchal society of myth and tradition, the society of Christendom; and the coming of the society of secular, rational mind, the modern society of history and science—Shakespeare, excepting Cervantes, was the first great writer to define history as a moral exercise of the literary imagination. While it would seem he did not deliberately do so, Shakespeare conceived that through fictive constructs man has the capacity to imagine history as the symbol of his existential possibilities. Shakespeare projected the making of the world by the mind of man as the meaning of history. If we regard the modern age and modern literature as originating in the age of Shakespeare and Sir Francis Bacon, we recognize how, if "covertly and by snatches" as Melville says, Shakespeare prophesies a great historical truth of modernity: the progressive act over a period of five centuries of internalizing history. A striking anticipation of how the growing will of the human mind to assume control of history will become both liberating and enslaving is anticipated in Hamlet's response to the command he receives from his father's ghost to rectify the history of a kingdom. Hamlet enters the mandate in "the book and volume of my brain," and struggling to repair the fracturing of time, experiences history as an agony of the consciousness.

Both in Philip C. Kolin's introductory essay to *Shakespeare and Southern Writers: A Study in Influence* and in the essays by his contributors on individual writers, we see a fulfillment of the Shakespearean suggestion of the psychic burden of history on the individual. Poignantly known to Simms, Henry Timrod, and Sidney Lanier (as Charles S. Watson, Christina Murphy, and Thomas Daniel Young show), the imposition of history on the consciousness was experienced in a more complicated and intimate way by Mark Twain. *Huckleberry Finn* not only satirizes the melodramatic theatrics of the nineteenth-century American stage but in drawing the portrait of con artists like the duke and the king makes a profoundly ironic commentary on the incapacity of the human mind to assume the burden of history. In the remaining studies in this provocative book Timothy Kevin Conley, Kelsie Harder, Mark Royden Winchell, and J. Madison Davis indicate how in still more complex ways the Shakespearean intimation of the psychic burden of history is reflected in William Faulkner, John Crowe Ransom, Robert Penn Warren, and Walker Percy. In these writers the theme of the southern self-consciousness of history as set forth in nineteenth-century figures like Simms and Mark Twain reaches fulfillment as the major subject of southern literature.

Lewis P. Simpson

Shakespeare and Southern Writers

Shakespeare and Southern Writers:
An Introduction

Philip C. Kolin

Shakespeare in the South: Essays on Performance (Jackson: University Press of Mississippi, 1983) has impressively documented Shakespeare's popularity as a playwright on both antebellum and modern southern stages. This volume, which might be regarded as a companion to that earlier collection, concentrates on Shakespeare's influence on selected southern authors and their response to him. The eight essays gathered here were written especially for this volume and examine Shakespeare's presence in the life and works of southern authors of the nineteenth and twentieth centuries. The collection explores specific points of indebtedness as well as larger thematic similarities uniting Shakespeare to southern writers. Major southern writers in this collection who were influenced by Shakespeare include Mark Twain, William Faulkner, John Crowe Ransom, and Robert Penn Warren. Identifying these figures as southern writers does not deny their national or even international reputations; instead, such a designation points to a shared heritage as well as to the significant ways in which these writers as a group responded to Shakespeare. Also heard in this collection are the voices of minor figures whose regional significance is major—Henry Timrod, Sidney Lanier, William Gilmore Simms. The reputation of the eighth figure, Walker Percy, is still in the making.

Specifically, this collection strives to accomplish two goals: (1) to provide a much needed account of Shakespeare's influence on the works of these eight authors; and (2) to assess Shakespeare's influence on southern letters in general. The second goal is achieved as readers compare and contrast the varied ways in which Shakespeare shaped the style, ideas, and critical manifestoes of southern literature.

No single work exists that exclusively considers Shakespeare's influence on southern authors as a group. Histories of southern literature mention Shakespeare in passing, if at all. That such a study is necessary cannot be denied when one recalls the pervasive influence Shakespeare has had on southern writers from Thomas Jefferson to Walker Percy. Attempts to survey that influence on individual authors must be judged as largely incomplete. One looks in vain for a comprehensive or even adequate analysis of the importance of Shakespeare in the works of any southern writer. A few examples will illustrate this deficiency. In reconstructing Twain's library, Alan Gribben (*Mark Twain's Library* [Boston, 1980]) catalogues the books Twain knew, including a large number of Shakespeare's plays. But Gribben, as well as John Baetzhold (*Mark Twain and John Bull* [Bloomington, Ind., 1970]), classifies rather than analyzes. We seek a satisfying understanding of Twain's knowledge of and response to Shakespeare. Likewise, no work on Faulkner, including Joseph Blotner's magisterial biography (*Faulkner: A Biography* [New York: Random House, 1974]), explores in depth Faulkner's indebtedness to Shakespeare for language, technique, or theme. For these as well as for other southern writers, one can point to a group of articles or, more likely, brief notes, where echoes—audible, faint, or imaginary—are brought to the reader's attention. These random instances, however, lack the continuity and coherence of a focused and sustained study. It is safe to conclude, I believe, that discussion of Shakespeare's influence on the work of most southern authors remains incomplete. This collection seeks in part to fill in necessary details for these eight authors.

I must point out, though, that this volume makes no claim to be a comprehensive study. Eight authors do not represent all of southern literature, nor do they include all of the southern authors who may have been influenced by Shakespeare. These eight figures were selected for this volume for the following reasons:

1. They are representative authors for various periods of southern literature—the early nineteenth century, the local color movement, the Age of the Fugitives–Agrarians, the modern novel.

2. Their works represent the widely different genres in which Shakespeare's influence was present—the lyric, the drama (comedy and tragedy), the novel, satire, and (especially intriguing) criticism.

3. The works of these eight authors offer a sustained and provable Shakespearean influence. Unquestionably other southern writers may have read Shakespeare and responded to the myths and mysteries he explored. For example, thanks to the work of meticulous scholars, we have firm evidence of Poe's use of and indebtedness to Shakespeare. But in many other cases we lack firm evidence to prove, or sometimes even to speculate, that Shakespearean language or cast of mind clearly surfaces in or shapes the work of, say, Flannery O'Connor, Eudora Welty, Richard Wright, or Willie Morris. Internal and external evidence establishes Shakespeare's influence in the works of the eight authors studied in this volume.

As the following summaries point out, the essays in this collection are as varied as they are complementary. Each strives to document and assess Shakespeare's influence; yet each approaches the topic from a different perspective. Some essays meticulously record Shakespearean allusions, characterizations, and dramatic techniques; several identify major Shakespearean models that southern authors used in fiction or drama. Most essays do not range over an author's entire canon but introduce selected texts for interpretation of the Shakespearean significance. These essays frequently delve into a particularly regional interpretation of Shakespeare's works—especially the sonnets—by southern critics and authors.

This collection begins appropriately with Charles S. Watson's essay on William Gilmore Simms. Among nineteenth-century men of letters, perhaps no one responded to or adapted Shakespeare more prolifically than Simms. Watson convincingly interprets this southern response to Shakespeare in Simms's work as editor, literary critic, theatre reviewer, and, most important, as novelist. As Watson points out, Simms "imitated Shakespearean characters from his earliest to his latest fictional works." Watson shows the mark of Falstaff on Captain Porgy, explains the influence of *Othello* on the plot and major characters of *Confession,* and assesses the Hamlet figures (and "anti-Hamlet characters") who populate Simms's works. But, as Watson rightly emphasizes, Simms did not borrow Shakespearean characters without altering them for his time and place. In his characterization of the Revolutionary War Captain Porgy, Simms "sacrifices the radicalness of Falstaff's cynicism for the geniality of Porgy's wisdom." Doubtless the dashes of the southern gentleman in Porgy helped the character to mellow. Most "provocative" is Simms's use of Hamlet, whose indecision he employed to characterize the indolent southern planters he found all around him, thus hoping to correct their faults by urging them to assume martial readiness. Translocated to a southern setting, Simms's Hamlet-figures are "bucolic" or "comic," weighted down by their "nervo-lymphatic temperament." As Watson perceptively concludes, "Hamlet provided Simms with an important key to understanding southern society."

Studying Shakespeare's influence upon Henry Timrod, hailed as the "Laureate of the Confederacy," Christina Murphy argues that "Shakespeare was Timrod's paradigm." In his verse, early and late, Timrod used Shakespearean models to present his views about poetry and about the southern ethos. In "A Vision," echoes of *A Midsummer Night's Dream* flow mellifluously through Timrod's imagery and metaphysical style, his character named Puck, and the pastoral locale. Like Shakespeare, Timrod lauds the ethereal gifts of poesy and surveys man's place in nature. Kindred spirits socially as well as poetically, Timrod and Shakespeare confronted "a culture of alienation." In a detailed commentary on Timrod's "Address Delivered at the Opening of the New Theatre at Richmond," Murphy shows how four Shakespearean characters are used to represent "a distinct perspective upon history which Timrod analyzes and compares to the present situations of his era." The first character in the "Address" is Miranda who symbolizes the brave innocence of the Old South. Next comes Lear who epitomizes the spiritual and social struggles which the South had to endure. In the figure of Hamlet Timrod found a model of the southerner "willing to sacrifice . . . life for the attainment of noble ideals," an interpretation of that character far different from Simms's. Finally, the Othello who appears in the "Address" raises questions about justice and racial issues in the South. Murphy thus reveals how Timrod profoundly and often relied on Shakespeare to be his "poetic guide."

In the next essay, Thomas Daniel Young explores Sidney Lanier's "deep and genuine appreciation of Shakespeare," as manifested in Lanier's Peabody Institute and Johns Hopkins lectures, sections of which appeared in *Shakespere and His Forerunners* and *The Science of English Verse.* Lanier wrote and lectured about Shakespeare all of his adult life. In a characteristic nineteenth-century vein, Lanier searched the plays for "an uplifting moral" and strove "to show Shakespeare as hero, humankind at the height of its development." Viewed from the vantage point of the late twentieth century, however, these lectures "are not reliable scholarship," Young admits. To be sure, Lanier was a "homemade scholar." But the lectures do reveal Lanier's infectious enthusiasm and his unbounded desire for knowledge about Shakespeare. No topic of scholarly inquiry appears to escape Lanier's notice. He presents biography, often fictionally recreated; explores the themes of friendship, loneliness, and betrayal in the sonnets; and studies Shakespearean characters' speech and accent, which Lanier claims do not represent real speech patterns but reflect "the emotions that underlie them." Charting the course of Shakespeare's work through a period of "youthful rioting" to a time of "single-passion tragedies" and finally to "the Heavenly Period," Lanier paid special attention to Shakespeare's verse, comparing it to music, devising metrical tests to reveal its power and majesty, and showing how Shakespeare was able "to balance artistically the oppositions of which verse is made." What he wrote and thought about Shakespeare tells us a great deal about the age in which Lanier lived.

Mark Twain's use and abuse of Shakespeare is the subject of the essay by Thomas J. Richardson. Surveying four representative Twain works, Richardson emphasizes how they "offer some general sense of Twain's ambivalent attitude toward Shakespeare and his works." Richardson's astute analysis reveals much about Twain's "divided sensibility." In *Julius Caesar Localized,* Twain's burlesque is "relatively mild." When Twain made a comic intrusion into *Hamlet,* adding to the cast of Shakespeare's play the bumptious foster brother of the prince, he was careful not "to alter Shakespeare's existing lines." Richardson argues that Twain's "most successful use of Shakespeare" is in chapter 21 of *The Adventures of Huckleberry Finn,* where the Duke delivers a comic version of Hamlet's famous soliloquy. Richardson mines the richness of that speech, interpreting its "originality and coherence" and studying its relationship to "the larger events of the novel." Richardson also asserts that Twain's "most direct" statement on Shakespeare occurs in *Is Shakespeare Dead?,* where Twain cynically contributes to the authorship controversy declaring Bacon's claims more justifiable than Shakespeare's. Although Twain's "basic approach to Shakespeare is irreverent," Richardson stresses that Twain still admired the plays and establishes that he knew them exceedingly well.

In a carefully documented essay, Timothy Kevin Conley gauges the rich and changing influence of Shakespeare on the life and the works of William Faulkner, one of the most famous southern authors to imbibe Shakespeare deeply. Conley assesses that influence by studying Faulkner's "growing awareness of the significance of the past—historical and literary." For Faulkner, he says, Shakespeare represented the burden of the past he had to acknowledge yet felt compelled to throw off. Shakespeare played a crucial role in Faulkner's "creative process," and was the yardstick by which Faulkner judged his own works; in effect, Shakespeare became Faulkner's casebook. Faulkner's appreciation for Shakespeare was inspired by his mother and by his early mentor, Phil Stone, both of whom contributed to an "unstructured course for his education." Conley devotes a great deal of attention to Shakespearean influence in Faulkner's early work to demonstrate how Faulkner's use of and response to Shakespeare evolved throughout his career. Conley notes that "a graph of the number of borrowings, echoes, and allusions would reveal that Shakespeare's presence is most often felt in the first half of Faulkner's career—particularly in *Soldier's Pay, Flags in the Dust, The Sound and the Fury,* and *Absalom, Absalom!*" Conley sees *Absalom, Absalom!* as especially important; "in terms of his use of and attitude toward Shakespeare *Absalom* marks the completion of one phase of Faulkner's career." In the novels immediately following *Absalom*—*Wild Palms, Go Down, Moses, The Unvanquished*—Faulkner suffered from external pressures, and here, Conley says, "Shakespeare provides only slogans and distant parallels." But in the fiction of his last two decades, Faulkner "refocuses his view of Shakespeare's comic plot." Conley observes that the "movement" in Faulkner's last works "reverses Shakespeare's: the historic sense postdates the tragic for Faulkner." At the end of his career, Faulkner did not struggle against the past or challenge Shakespeare; he endured with him.

The following essays by Kelsie B. Harder and Mark Royden Winchell concentrate on the reception of Shakespeare by two of the most illustrious of Nashville's Fugitive poets. Harder studies John Crowe Ransom; Winchell examines Robert Penn Warren. "Shakespeare was a most proper concern for the Nashville group," Harder rightly observes. He finds that strictures leveled against Shakespeare by Ransom originated in his own sense of southernness, although that southernness "does not easily surface." Decrying the sentimentality, emotionalism, and violence which contributed to the tragedy of the Civil War, Ransom viewed the southerner as "a J. Alfred Prufrock in ante-bellum dress." As Harder points out, Ransom thought such individuals needed to "develop an ironic and self-deprecating posture in order to survive socially." Because of his apollonian rather than dionysian predisposition, Ransom preferred the metaphysical wit—the irony—of John Donne over the seductive emotional appeal of Shakespeare. Ransom's formalism thus censured as poetic weaknesses the romantic traits he found in Shakespeare's sonnets. Ransom therefore concluded that few of the sonnets were "well built," that the form "was too small to hold Shakespeare's imagery," and that, most unacceptable of all, Shakespeare "indulged in a whining and evasive self-pity that hardly is justified." In five words, Harder explains the reason behind Ransom's ire: "Shakespeare was not an Agrarian."

Not all members of the Nashville group were of Ransom's opinion. In examining Robert Penn Warren's critical response to Shakespeare, Mark Royden Winchell suggests that Warren possessed a considerably more romantic and gothic sensibility than did his mentor Ransom. Specifically, Winchell cites Warren's essay on "Pure and Impure Poetry" and the discussion of "Cleopatra's Lament" in *Understanding Poetry*. Winchell then examines what might be regarded as Shakespearean excesses in the imagery of Warren's early verse, tracing the Shakespearean allusions and themes occurring up to the publication of the original version of Warren's *Brothers to Dragons* (1953). In considering the Shakespearean influence on Warren's fiction, Winchell evaluates the Shakespearean criticism at the heart of Warren's second novel, *At Heaven's Gate,* and finds that Warren's most famous novel, *All the King's Men,* is also his most Shakespearean. Acknowledging the frequent parallels between *Julius Caesar* and the plot and theme of *All the King's Men,* Winchell finds fruitful comparisons between Jack Burden and Hamlet, protagonist of another Shakespearean play of politics and power.

In the last essay of this collection, J. Madison Davis examines the use of Shakespeare by one of the South's most respected contemporary novelists, Walker Percy. Although Percy's own critical pronouncements question the merit of allusion and metaphor, his fiction—especially *Lancelot,* the subject of Davis's attention—shows the influence of a "list of literary and philosophical works," including those of Shakespeare. The references to Shakespearean works in the novel, Davis persuasively argues, are neither "casual" nor "offhand." They "occur frequently and contribute much to the beauty and complexity" of the novel. In particular, Davis finds that Percy shapes his works of fiction with allusions from two of Shakespeare's "plays of self-discovery," *Henry IV, Part I* and *King Lear.* In confronting the "lack of heroism" in the modern world, Percy's protagonist, Lancelot Lamar, carves a career "like Hotspur's." His friend and confessor, Father John, is likened by Walker Percy to Prince Hal, the man whose vocation is unexpected. But Lancelot's story "can be interpreted as a tragedy," and Davis investigates the parallels between the situation of the southern aristocrat plunged into darkness and despair by his family and the plight of King Lear. Both men inhabit "an imbecile universe," father "three daughters," realize that "their self-deceptions are destroyed," endure the frenzy of a storm, and are consequently "reduced to madness." In his "layering of the past on the present," as Davis points out, Percy achieves a universality in his fiction, showing how, by metaphor, individuals can be Lears, Hals, or Hotspurs and thus recognize the bitter price that can be paid for attempting to live up to old ideals and not develop new ones. Indebted to Shakespeare as were Simms and Timrod, Percy uses allusions to the plays combined with other echoes, ancient and recent, to formulate a message for a modern world "tangled in a web of mythologies."

As these essays show individually and collectively, *Shakespeare and Southern Writers: A Study in Influence* uncovers intriguing parallels and relationships between Shakespeare and representative major and minor southern authors of the nineteenth and twentieth centuries. The work in this collection is both necessary and new. Scholars in American literature, Shakespearean studies, and southern culture now have a single collection of essays which documents what has been often thought but less often substantiated. Shakespeare's role in the work of the eight authors in this collection is an important one, as each of the essays impressively proves. But the essays do more than document the fact that Shakespeare's work was known and used by these eight authors; they also show how Shakespeare was interpreted from a distinctly regional perspective. Shakespeare certainly influenced southern writers, and they in turn have influenced the way readers will continue to respond to him.

Simms's Use of Shakespearean Characters

Charles S. Watson

In analyzing the flowering of southern literature in the twentieth century, critics have often observed that modern influences from outside the region have contributed greatly. What they have underemphasized is a comparable debt owed to the past. In drawing on the classic authors of earlier centuries southern writers have demonstrated once more their talent for appreciating the values of older times. Shakespeare's inspiration, the epitome of this influence from the past, begins emphatically with one of the first important writers of the South.

The most representative man of letters of the antebellum South, William Gilmore Simms, notably exemplifies the veneration of Shakespeare felt by writers of that time and place. Simms shared the Romantic period's fascination with Shakespeare and he revealed its impact on his writing throughout his career. When he composed his tribute to the classic writers of English literature, "Heads of the Poets," he demonstrated his esteem for Shakespeare by devoting two sections to him.[1] Finally, the most significant influence of Shakespeare is Simms's use of famous Shakespearean characters in his own writing. Before examining that influence, however, it will be helpful to note the extent and variety of Simms's interest in Shakespeare.

Epigraphs from Shakespeare's plays are by far the most numerous in the chapter headings of Simms's novels. According to Grace Whaley, Shakespeare appears there more than any other author, with a total of 120 epigraphs in eighteen novels. There is a particularly large number of such epigraphs in Simms's novel about a traveling Shakespearean actor, *Border Beagles*.[2] Characters such as Captain Porgy, Simms's expert on Shakespeare, quote from the Bard knowingly and frequently. In *Woodcraft* Captain Porgy expresses his philosophy of serenity amidst the chaos of the post-Revolutionary South, when he quotes from *The Taming of the Shrew:* "Let the world slide!—

Sessa" ("Induction," scene 1). Characters also repeat well-known sentiments of Shakespearean characters. Echoing the words of Shylock, Hurricane Nell of *Eutaw* objects to the social persecution she suffers: "Do I not think as other women, feel as other women?"[3] (*The Merchant of Venice,* 3.1).

Among nineteenth-century American authors who wrote about Shakespeare, like Emerson in his *Representative Men* (1844), Simms was unusual in undertaking the task of editor. He made a bold foray into Shakespearean scholarship with his edition of Shakespeare's apocryphal plays: *A Supplement to the Plays of William Shakespeare* (1848), which contains such plays as *Locrine* and *Sir John Oldcastle.* This volume was the first critical reprinting of the seven apocryphal plays in over sixty years, following the edition of 1780 issued by Edmund Malone.[4] Simms revealed the creative writer's approach clearly in his introduction. He was primarily interested in seeing Shakespeare's apprenticeship in the early works attributed to him. In this way, he contended, we can gain a greater understanding of the growth of the great dramatist. Simms defended his printing of these plays by saying that they would enable us to follow Shakespeare in "his workshop."[5]

Though Simms proves his knowledge of Shakespearean criticism in the introduction, the edition itself shows that he was not a professional scholar. When C.F. Tucker Brooke edited *The Shakespeare Apocrypha* (1908), he listed all of Simms's conjectures and discussed some in his notes, calling Simms an unquestioning follower of Edmund Malone. Edd Winfield Parks in his *William Gilmore Simms as Literary Critic* disagreed in part with this wholesale dismissal of Simms. He said that Simms relied on other editors besides Malone, and also pointed out that Simms made changes of his own in the texts, though he was not scrupulous about noting all of them.[6]

Simms was a great devotee of Shakespearean acting. He attended the theatre often and evaluated the great actors of his time for Charleston newspapers. In particular, he reviewed the acting of Charles Kean, Thomas Cooper, and Edwin Forrest in Shakespearean roles.[7] On a visit to New Orleans in 1831 he reported seeing Charles Kean in *Othello;* and in the February

(1831) issue of the *Southern Literary Journal* he appraised John W. Vandenhoff's performance as Hamlet in Charleston. In *Border Beagles,* comic actor Tom Horsey gives imitations of the famous Shakespearean actors whom Simms had seen, and in the process evidently expresses Simms's judgments. Besides speaking in "the guttural growl of Forrest," Horsey mimics Kean's deformed visage and Cooper's lugubrious whinings. He also delivers recitations from *Macbeth, Hamlet,* and *Richard III.*[8] In addition, Simms composed a version of *Timon of Athens* for his friend, Edwin Forrest, but it was never produced.[9]

Simms's most significant borrowing from Shakespeare is his use of Shakespearean characters as models for his own. In this practice he employed a technique evident in other Romantic novelists such as Scott, Cooper, and Melville. Simms imitated Shakespearean characters in his earliest on through his latest fictional works. Throughout his border romances, Shakespearean parallels appear frequently. In *Guy Rivers* (1834), Simms compares the title character, a murderer-outlaw, to Macbeth. In *Richard Hurdis* (1838), he likens the vision of a spectre which a poor white sees after killing a young man to Macbeth's vision of Banquo.[10] In his version of the Kentucky Tragedy, *Beauchampe* (1842), he parallels Col. Sharpe's seduction of the hero's wife with Falstaff's wooing in *The Merry Wives of Windsor.* Finally, in his next-to-last novel, *Voltmeier* (1869), he compares the title character to Prospero when the planter transforms the mountain wilderness into a beautifully cultivated estate.[11]

Of Simms's many imitations of Shakespearean characters four examples are most noteworthy. In his treatments of Falstaff, Othello, Iago, and Hamlet, Simms adapted the great creations of Shakespeare for his own purposes, as Melville did for his Hamlet-like characterization of Pierre. Melville transferred Shakespearean characters to an American milieu in *Moby Dick* and *Pierre,* and Simms followed suit in his own fiction. His adaptations were strongly affected by the culture and history of the South, and revealed his increasing skill and insight in employing Shakespearean characters as models.

Simms's best-known use of a Shakespearean character is his portrayal of Porgy of the South Carolina Partisans. This character, who appears in five of Simms's Revolutionary romances, is clearly modeled after Falstaff. Porgy is fat, a lover of food, and an eloquent talker. As Falstaff does in Shakespeare's plays, Porgy takes a dual role, as military man and as suitor of women. In the four romances occurring during the Revolution, Porgy plays the former role; in the romance of the post-Revolutionary period, *Woodcraft,* he takes the latter part. Like Falstaff, Porgy is surrounded by a band of good fellows. Among them are George Dennison, his poet; young Lance Frampton, who resembles Prince Hal in scenes where Porgy chides him humorously; and his slave retainers, led by his body servant Tom. Porgy's remarks frequently recall those of Falstaff. After a French officer insults Porgy's equipment in *The Partisan,* for example, Porgy ridicules his thinness, as Falstaff derided Prince Hal's slight dimensions.[12]

There are several explicit references to Falstaff in the passages presenting Porgy. When Porgy makes his initial entrance in *The Partisan* (1835), Simms comments that Porgy amused himself by talking about food "as Falstaff discoursed of his own cowardice without feeling it"[13] (*Henry IV,* Part I, 2.4). In the finale of Simms's Revolutionary epic, *Eutaw* (1855), Porgy compares himself directly to Falstaff. He likens his capture of some docile Irish soldiers to the conquest of Sir Coleville of the Dale by "the fat knight of Eastcheap." Porgy reports that he spoke to the Irishmen in Falstaff's words: " 'Like kind fellows ye gave yourselves away, and I thank ye for yourselves' " (Henry IV, Part II, 4.3). He did not have to sweat for them any more than "Sir John" did, he declares.[14]

Simms does not let Falstaff dominate Porgy, however, and his portrayal of this character is similar to all of his best adaptations of Shakespearean characters in that he altered the original model substantially to shape a clearly identifiable American character. Hampton Jarrell has demonstrated convincingly that in the overall portrayal of Porgy Simms modified his resemblance to Falstaff with the traits of a Southern gentleman.[15]

The process of alteration can be seen distinctly in Porgy's first appearance in the Revolutionary series, because Simms substantially changed the characterization when he revised *The Partisan* in 1854. When Simms reissued his novels in the collected edition of his works, he made extensive revisions in some of them. His alterations of Porgy in *The Partisan,* which lessened the Falstaffian parallel, are his most felicitous corrections. As time passed Simms's conception of Porgy changed; he wished to make him a more important person, consistent with his impressive role in *Woodcraft* (1852) as the representative southern planter. In the revision of *The Partisan,* Porgy becomes a more complex, rounded character, not merely a southern version of Falstaff. According to Paula Dean, only in *The Partisan,* revised, does the reader discover "precisely what Porgy looks like or what makes him behave as he does." No longer only a "squire," he becomes a lieutenant. His sociability appears early in the novel now, seen particularly in his friendship with George Dennison. Above all he is a gentleman, both by birth and education.[16] Displaying his erudition, Porgy cites "Menenius Agrippa," in defending the size of his belly (*Coriolanus,* 1.1). No reference to the Shakespearean character is given in the first version of this passage.[17]

Consistent with his newly conceived divergence from Falstaff, Porgy philosophizes in a different tone from his Shakespearean antecedent. As a Southern planter, Porgy consistently takes a humorous tone, rather than the worldly-wise one of Falstaff's disquisition on honor. Porgy's leading function in Simms's Revolutionary romances is to comment perceptively on a principal theme of the novel. He comments on a main theme of *The Partisan,* the search for security, as seen in the futile effort of some Carolinians to find security among the British. Porgy philosophizes on how foolish man's obsession with security really is. When his friend Dr. Oakenburg complains about the dangers of the swamp, saying that he was promised "perfect security" if he joined the Partisans, Porgy points to a nearby snake and says there is little security of any kind until dinner is over. Only then, he proclaims, do we know "as much security as life knows." When Porgy has finished his terrapin soup, he exclaims with deep satisfaction and tranquility, "So much is secure of life."[18] In his characterization of Porgy, Simms sacrifices the radical quality of Falstaff's cynicism for the geniality of Porgy's wisdom.

When in 1841 Simms turned from historical novels about the Indians and the Revolution to the psychological novel, he selected the cast of characters in *Othello* as his models. *Othello* was one of Simms's favorite plays; he called it "one of the most noble of all moralities" and quoted from it often in his letters.[19] *Confession* is the story of a husband, Edward Clifford, who becomes suspicious of the love of his Desdemona-like wife for a young man, William Edgerton. In the end, Clifford poisons his supposedly unfaithful wife and suffers agonizing remorse.

Simms makes the comparison to Shakespeare's characters explicit by references to them and by quotations from the play. Edward, fully recognizing his jealousy of Edgerton, calls himself an "Othello" and says, in a soliloquy when he departs for Alabama, Edgerton will have even more opportunity to spend long hours with his wife. After he poisons Julia Edward terms his lament "Othello's apostrophe." He exclaims: "My wife! my wife! What wife—I have no wife!/ Oh, insupportable—O heavy hour!" (5.2).[21]

Simms employs the Othello-figure of this novel to offer his own explanation of the Moor's fall. Clifford remarks that Othello's flaw was not really jealousy but outraged pride which led too promptly to fatal action. Clifford asserts that Othello was one of "the least jealous of human natures"; he had sufficient "proofs" to deceive any jury, and self-esteem caused him to act precipitously.[21] Clifford himself admits his own jealousy freely and thus distinguishes himself from Simms's conception of Othello. This interpretation of Othello resembles that of Coleridge, who said that the Moor killed Desdemona not out of jealousy but because of a conviction forced upon him by the superhuman trickery of Iago.[22]

The Iago of *Confession* turns out to be a much more interesting creation than the others whom Simms based on the *dramatis personae* of *Othello*. Nevertheless, two critics have written that Simms's version of *Othello* lacks an equivalent of Iago. According to William P. Trent, Simms felt that Othello was jealous only because he was "practiced upon by an Iago," and decided to write another version, presenting the husband as moved only by "inward workings." J. V. Ridgely stated that there was no Iago working on Edward Clifford.[23] These are mistaken views, however, because Clifford does have his Iago.

Frank Kingsley is the Iago of this novel. He seems a well-meaning fellow who wants to help Clifford, yet the effect of his words and actions is to make Clifford more suspicious and to alienate him from his wife. Although in talking with Clifford about his wife Kingsley claims that he does not want to make him suspicious, he succeeds in fanning the flames of jealousy. He says that a cunning fellow like Edgerton may rob a man's affections, but "I do not intimate—I would not willingly believe—that she would submit to anything of the sort." Kingsley takes Clifford away from his wife in order to visit a gambling den and urges him on, repeating Iago's famous words, "Put money in thy own purse" (1.3).[24]

Simms alters his Iago radically by making him a humorous character. He does this by adding to the Shakespearean model the indigenous material of Southwestern humor. Adopting the guise of a humorous Kentuckian, for example, Kingsley relates a long-winded story to Julia's mother, thus allowing Edward and Julia time to elope. He resembles an eccentric such as Longstreet's Ned Brace of *Georgia Scenes,* who assumed any character his humor required. Kingsley also imitates a Texas braggart. Describing his future projects in Texas, he says that when he gets among the Cumanches he will become the first prince "Sans Souci," with "a code of laws and constitution to suit any particular humor."[25] Throughout the novel Kingsley breeds jealousy and contributes to the final tragedy, but under Simms's pen he does so as a carefree American buffoon.

Simms's use of Hamlet in creating characters is his most provocative borrowing from Shakespeare. With Shakespeare's philosophic prince as the prototype, Simms analyzed the leading social class of the South, the planters, whom he saw as suffering from Hamlet's besetting sin, indecision. In his portrayal of the representative planter, Porgy of *Woodcraft,* as a Hamlet figure, he endeavored to dissect the breed of mankind that he knew best and that he saw as directing his section's fortunes. Simms had thought long and hard about Hamlet, had written about him in an essay, and had observed Hamlet types all around him before he presented his literary version of a southern Hamlet.

Simms considered "The Moral Character of Hamlet" to be his best piece of Shakespearean criticism. Here Simms built on the late eighteenth-century tradition of analyzing Shakespearean characters psychologically.[26] This essay was published first in four issues of *The Orion* (March, April, May, June 1844). Later Simms presented it in two lectures, carrying the same title, at the Smithsonian Institute on February 13 and 15, 1854.[27] In this study Simms expressed the Romantic view that Hamlet's will was defective. He stressed Hamlet's indecision and impulsive action as his principal traits, and concluded that Hamlet could act only when circumstances impelled him. In this analysis, he again expressed views close to those expounded by Coleridge, who argued that Shakespeare's message in *Hamlet* is that action is the chief end of existence.[28] Coleridge saw in Hamlet an over-balance of the contemplative faculty, which prevented forthright action. As a result, he said, Hamlet finally accomplishes his goal by mere accident.[29]

Hamlet fascinated Simms because the author observed contemporary Hamlets all around him. In "The Moral Character of Hamlet" this native Charlestonian wrote that indecisive men like Hamlet appear only "in *old* communities" such as Boston and Charleston, not in Texas, where action is indispensable.[30] What disturbed Simms most was that he recognized Hamlet in his closest associates, who should be providing the vigorous leadership that his state and region sorely needed as the sectional controversy intensified. Simms's criticism included his closest friend, James H. Hammond, a former governor of South Carolina who withdrew from political activities after being involved in a personal scandal and remained away for an extended period. Hammond mulled over philosophic subjects on his Savannah River plantation for ten years before returning to active political life in 1857. Clement Eaton called him "the Hamlet of the Old South" because of his indecision in political matters.[31] Simms often tried to arouse him to action and in 1849 warned him, "Remember Hamlet—'whose native hue of resolution / Was sicklied o'er by the pale cast of thought.' "[32]

Being a novelist, Simms turned to fiction in his attempt to correct the faults of his fellow southerners. Falstaff is the main model for Porgy in the novels set during the Revolutionary War, but he is replaced by Hamlet in the postwar novel of peacetime, *Woodcraft,* which focuses on the life of the planter. Here Simms portrays Porgy, the representative planter, as self-indulgent, chronically ruminant, and dilatory—in short, a bucolic Hamlet.

Porgy resembles Hamlet, first of all, because he is a specimen of the philosophic man. Throughout the novel he philosophizes on life, enemies, and women. He shows his likeness to Shakespeare's hero more pointedly when he longs to escape the torments of this world. Porgy's meditative qualities take a melancholy turn when he returns to his debt-ridden plantation after the war. He listens to his overseer describe his financial plight and puffs on his pipe, a repeated sign of cloudy meditation. "To smoke is to contemplate," he says. As he lies down to sleep in a bare bedchamber his despondency increases and he believes it would not be difficult now to die. He thinks to himself: "To die, was to escape the cares, the troubles and the humiliations to which he felt himself unequal, and which he now felt to be inevitable from life."[33] This is Porgy's paraphrasing of a passage from Hamlet's "To be or not to be" soliloquy:

> To die, to sleep—
> No more, and by a sleep to say we end
> The heart-ache and the thousand natural shocks
> That flesh is heir to; 'tis a consummation
> Devoutly to be wish'd. (3.1)[34]

Simms's analysis of Hamlet in his essay applies as well to his characterization of Porgy in *Woodcraft.* Both exhibit indecision as well as the tendency to act only in an emergency. Significantly, Simms attributes one cause of Hamlet's indecision to his *"fatness."* Simms believed that obesity increased what he called Hamlet's "lymphatic," or sluggish humor. As evidence of Hamlet's heaviness he quotes his mother's remark in the fencing scene, "He's fat, and scant of breath" (5.2).[35] It can hardly be claimed that this single comment advances our understanding of

Hamlet's character, but it does illuminate Simms's depiction of the dilatory planter as a fat man, as well as his misunderstanding of Elizabethan idiom. "Fat" in Shakespeare's play may mean "soft" or "sweaty," but not "obese."

In his provocative book, *Cavalier and Yankee: The Old South and the American National Character,* William R. Taylor wrote that in his lectures on Hamlet delivered in the middle 1850s Simms was thinking of the indecisive southerner when he analyzed Hamlet. Simms, he concluded, viewed Hamlet as "Porgy grown anxious" and confronted by an uncontrollable "destiny."[36] Taylor's comparison of Porgy and the Hamlet of Simms's 1854 lectures is noteworthy, but Taylor fails to note Porgy's likeness to Hamlet in *Woodcraft.* Simms had already connected the two in his characterization of the philosophic planter in the novel of 1852.

Simms reenforces his attack on the Hamlet-like flaws of Porgy in *Woodcraft* by presenting anti-Hamlets, characters who—like Fortinbras—do not spend time in contemplation when action is called for. Among them is Arthur Eveleigh, who courts a young woman resolutely and emerges as the future model planter who will lack the foibles of the comic Porgy. Early in the story Arthur demonstrates the proper qualifications of an ideal southern leader. When he and his mother are ambushed by outlaws, Arthur learns quickly the Partisan tactic of woodcraft and helps drive the outlaws off. Simms comments that after impulsively shooting an outlaw Arthur might have congratulated himself in "the language of Hamlet—'praised be rashness for it'" (5.2). Simms had quoted the same line in his essay on Hamlet, in discussing his impulsive action under stress.[37] When he uses it in *Woodcraft,* he does so without any disapproval. Such a deed is the antithesis of Hamlet's usual behavior and Simms does not hesitate to approve "rashness" when the circumstances call for prompt action. On the same page he appends another pertinent quotation from *Hamlet* to praise Arthur's immediate response:

> Our indiscretion sometimes serves us well
> When our deep plots do pail (5.2).

Simms alters drastically the Hamlet-model in characterizing

Porgy. He presents his Hamlet not as a tragic figure but as a comic one and satirizes him roundly, hoping in this way to reform the southern planter. For the plot he draws on *The Merry Wives of Windsor* to show the indecisive man's dilemma, rather than the conflict in Hamlet between revenge and conscience. Porgy cannot make up his mind which widow to marry; he delays interminably, and in the long run fails to gain the hand of either. The consequences of his delay are humiliation and philosophic resignation. Here Simms wishes to show the southern planter the disastrous results of indecision and thereby persuades him to change his ways.

The antidote to Hamlet's indecision, according to Simms, is the military spirit. As a historical novelist, Simms found his exemplars in the glorious past, not in the decaying present. He especially admired civilian-soldiers such as General Charles Cotesworth Pinckney, Porgy's lawyer in *Woodcraft,* who maintained their military vigor in peacetime. At the end of *Woodcraft* Porgy returns to his warlike habits with great success. He does not retaliate against his creditor's attempt to seize his plantation until the emergency provokes him to action, but when he does he is fully successful in regaining possession of his land. Porgy implements the Partisan tactic of surprise and puts the enemy to rout. Simms thinks that southerners have fallen into lassitude after their victories in war. The remedy for their Hamlet-like languor on the peacetime plantation is a return to military decisiveness.[38]

Simms's view of the southern planter as a Hamlet figure is supported by others. Under the heading, "From Hotspur to Hamlet," William R. Taylor traces the appearance of these two personality types in antebellum life and literature. He finds that economic decline in the old seaboard states of the South produced many atavists of Hamlet. Mary Boykin Chesnutt in her *Diary of Dixie* saw a decline in vigor after the Revolutionary generation. She observed that latter-day planters were slow to move. They were wonderful for a short spurt, but then liked to rest.[39]

Simms made one more significant use of the Hamlet figure in his last Revolutionary romance, *Joscelyn,* which was published in 1867 during the turbulent period of Reconstruction. Throughout his series of Revolutionary tales, Simms had been concerned continually with the man caught between the two warring sides of the Revolution. The decision of which side to choose was a widespread dilemma faced by Americans afraid of losing their property but secretly backing the cause of independence. James Fenimore Cooper presents this issue in *The Spy,* which is laid in the no man's land between the patriot and loyalist sides. Simms also concentrates on the man pulled both ways; the central character of *The Partisan,* Col. Walton, undergoes an internal struggle before committing himself to independence. Showing the persistence of the Hamlet figure in his thinking, Simms patterns his man-in-the-middle in *Joscelyn* on Hamlet.

Walter Dunbar is the son of a fiery old Tory in this story about the beginning of the Revolution in South Carolina and Georgia in 1775. Walter admires the purpose of the patriot side but acquiesces to his father's demand that he support the crown. His attempt to resolve the dilemma is futile, and he takes on the traits of Hamlet. When he rises to speak at the assembly in Augusta to argue the case for loyalty, he is pitifully ineffective because of his uncertainty. Listening to him is his foil in the novel, an anti-Hamlet figure named Stephen Joscelyn, who chooses the patriot cause and says that Walter has spoken like Hamlet, who forgot the best parts of his speech to the ghost because of his fright (4–5).[40]

By his later vacillation, which finally results in his utter disgrace, Walter continues to resemble Hamlet. In an analysis of Walter's character Simms detects the lymphatic temperament, the same weakness he had attributed to Hamlet in "The Moral Character of Hamlet." He describes Walter: "Of nervolymphatic temperament, he could arrive at conclusions, *but never in time,* and, with a certain consciousness of this, he was apt to be equally slow and precipitate in action; to hesitate where he should have leapt, and to rush headlong just where he should pause to survey and consider. He was never just where he should be in the moment of action."[41] This judgment of Walter is shown to be accurate at the end of the novel. Forced to deliver letters from his father to loyalist leaders in the highlands of

South Carolina, Walter is caught off guard when taken before the ruthless Tory leader, Col. Thomas Browne. Though the letters are not meant for Browne, Walter hesitates timorously when the Tory demands them. Browne knocks him to the ground, seizes the letters, and leaves Walter humiliated. In Simms's eyes the fate of the weak, Hamlet-like man is ignominious defeat. Those who wavered between the two sides in the Revolution became helpless victims.

There is good reason to conclude that in presenting a Hamlet-like character in *Joscelyn,* Simms was issuing a warning to the new generation arising after the Civil War. As in his previous Revolutionary romances, he intended a contemporary application for this tale of the past. Specifically, Simms's postbellum writings evinced an increasing concern with the education and moral development of youth. Like Robert E. Lee and other southerners after 1865, he turned his attention to the younger generation which had succeeded the old regime. In his late romance, *Voltmeier* (1869), Simms presents the marriage of a young lawyer to a refined maiden of the Blue Ridge mountains. Their auspicious union forecasts symbolically a better future for that region of the South. In his last public address, "The Sense of the Beautiful" (1870), Simms dealt with the proper education of young people. He said that appreciation of the beautiful would furnish youth with the spiritual strength to overcome destructive passions.[42]

In accord with his concern about the rising generation, the widower Simms had his own children to consider. While composing *Joscelyn* in 1867, he wrote his eldest son, Gilmore, that he could no longer look after him. He advised him to "assert the will," be prompt in action, and not "desultory" in mood. This last failing had made "our people" worthless, he believed.[43] In the aftermath of the Civil War Simms saw the Hamlet-like disposition as still posing a grave threat. This time, however, he focused on the new generation, which he believed should provide bold speakers on current issues. Thus he presented as the object lesson in *Joscelyn* the indecisive young lawyer, Walter Dunbar, whose Hamlet-like temporizing should be avoided at all cost.

Simms was singularly equipped to draw on Shakespeare's

treasures because of his thorough acquaintance with Shakespearean plays, acting, and scholarship. Among his many adaptations of Shakespeare's characters to enhance the portrayal of the figures in his own works, his treatment of Hamlet is most noteworthy. His essay on Hamlet and his use of types and antitypes in fiction show clearly that Hamlet provided Simms with an important key to understanding southern society. Because Simms was one of those interpreters who looked unfavorably on Hamlet's character, he used the Hamlet type as an instrument for criticizing the ineffectual planter who retreated into thought when he should have been up and about. Hence, for example, he satirized the philosohic Porgy of *Woodcraft*. The antidote for the southerner's incertitude was the martial spirit, best exemplified in the American Revolution. Thus in *Joscelyn* Simms contrasted the vacillation of Walter Dunbar with Stephen Joscelyn's firm decision to join the patriot cause. Simms castigated Hamlet-like procrastination from one generation to another, because he shared fully the South's traditional admiration of military boldness.

NOTES

1. William Gilmore Simms, *Poems Descriptive, Dramatic, Legendary and Contemplative*, 2 vols. (New York: Redfield, 1853), 2:155. This poem was first published in *Graham's* 33 (Sept. 1848): 170–171.

2. Grace W. Whaley, " A Note on Simms's Novels," *AL* 2 (1930): 173–174.

3. *Woodcraft* (1854; reprint, Spartanburg, S.C.: The Reprint Co., 1976), p. 118 and *Eutaw* (1856; reprint, Spartanburg, S.C.: The Reprint Co., 1976), p. 69. For Simms's paraphrasing of Shakespeare, see C. Hugh Holman, "Simms and the British Dramatists," *PMLA* 65 (June 1950): 350.

4. Alfred Van Rensselaer Westfall, *American Shakespearean Criticism* (New York: The H. W. Wilson Co., 1939), 138.

5. *A Supplement to the Plays of William Shakspeare* (1848; reprint, Auburn and Rochester: Alden and Beardsley, 1855), 8.

6. Edd Winfield Parks, *William Gilmore Simms as Literary Critic* (Athens: University of Georgia Press, 1961), 135n., 80.

7. Charles S. Watson, *Antebellum Charleston Dramatists* (University: University of Alabama Press, 1976), 118–119.

8. Miriam J. Shillingsburg, "Simms's Review of Shakespeare on the Stage," *Tennessee Studies in Literature* 16 (1971): 121–123, 124–125, 130.

9. *The Letters of William Gilmore Simms*, ed. Mary C. Simms Oliphant, Alfred Taylor Odell, and T. C. Duncan Eaves, 5 vols. (Columbia: University of South Carolina Press, 1952–56), 3: 202, 215.

10. Edward P. Vandiver, "Simms's Border Romances and Shakespeare," *SQ* 5 (Spring 1954): 132.

11. William Gilmore Simms, *Beauchampe* (1856; reprint, New York: A. C. Arm-

strong, 1882), 284. The two novels, *Charlemont* and *Beauchampe,* appeared first as one work, *Beauchampe,* in 1842. *Voltmeier, or The Mountain Men* (1869; reprint, Columbia: University of South Carolina Press, 1969), 331.

12. Hugh W. Heatherington, Introduction to *Cavalier of Old South Carolina* (Chapel Hill: University of North Carolina Press, 1966), 24.

13. William Gilmore Simms, *The Partisan* (1854); reprint, Spartanburg, S.C.: The Reprint Co., 1976), 110.

14. *Eutaw,* 351.

15. Hampton Jarrell, "Falstaff and Simms's Porgy," *AL* 3 (May 1931): 204–212.

16. Paula Fix Dean, "Revisions in the Revolutionary War Novels of William Gilmore Simms" (Ph.D. dissertation, Auburn University, 1971), 264.

17. *The Partisan,* 347; first edition (2 vols., 1835; reprint, Ridgewood, N.J., 1968), 2: 105.

18. *The Partisan,* 13, 364.

19. Parks, 77.

20. *Confession* (1841; reprint, New York: A. C. Armstrong, 1882), 275, 367.

21. Ibid., 135–136.

22. Augustus Ralli, *A History of Shakespearian Criticism,* 2 vols. (London: Oxford University Press, 1932), 1: 139.

23. William P. Trent, *William Gilmore Simms* (1892; reprint, New York: Greenwood Press, 1969), 122; and J. V. Ridgely, *William Gilmore Simms* (New York: Twayne, 1962), 85.

24. *Confession,* 320, 203.

25. Ibid., 205.

26. Westfall, 231–232.

27. "The Moral Character of Hamlet," *The Orion* 4 (March, April, May, June 1844): 41–51, 76–89, 105–119, 179–194, *Letters,* 3: 280n.; Parks, pp. 75, 133n.

28. Ralli, 1: 132.

29. Samuel Taylor Coleridge, "Hamlet," in *The Literary Remains of Samuel Taylor Coleridge,* (1836; reprint, New York: AMS Press, 1967), 204–207; Arthur M. Eastman, *A Short History of Shakespearean Criticism* (New York: Random House, 1968), pp. 70–71.

30. "The Moral Character of Hamlet," *The Orion* 4 (March 1844): 44–45.

31. Clement Eaton, *The Mind of the Old South* (Baton Rouge: Louisiana State University Press, 1964), 21.

32. *Letters,* 2: 488. Simms paraphrases from the "To be or not to be" soliloquy (*Hamlet,* 3.1).

33. *Woodcraft,* 186, 198. For further discussion of Porgy as Hamlet-like philosopher, see my introduction to the edition of *Woodcraft* (New Haven: New College and University Press, 1983).

34. *Hamlet,* 3.1, *The Riverside Shakespeare,* ed. G. Blakemore Evans (Boston: Houghton, Mifflin, 1974).

35. "The Moral Character of Hamlet," *The Orion* 4 (March 1844): 47.

36. See "From Falstaff to Hamlet," in William R. Taylor, *Cavalier and Yankee: The Old South and the American National Character* (New York: George Braziller, 1961), 291–297.

37. *Woodcraft,* 95; "The Moral Character of Hamlet," *The Orion* 4 (June 1844): 189.

38. For a full-scale treatment of the South's martial spirit see John Hope Franklin, *The Militant South, 1800–1861* (Cambridge: Harvard University Press, 1956).

39. Taylor, pp. 160–162.

40. *Joscelyn; A Tale of the Revolution* (1867; Columbia: University of South Carolina Press, 1975). This is the Centennial Simms Edition, with introduction and explanatory notes by Stephen E. Meats and text established by James B. Meriwether.

41. *Joscelyn,* 178.

42. "The Sense of the Beautiful" (Charleston: Walker, Evans, and Cogswell, 1870).

43. *Letters,* 5: 70 (July 13, 1867).

The Artistic Design of Societal Commitment: Shakespeare and the Poetry of Henry Timrod

Christina Murphy

Henry Timrod's reputation as "the Laureate of the Confederacy"[1] is based upon a group of poems—"Ethnogenesis," "The Cotton Boll," "Carolina," "Charleston," "Address Delivered at the Opening of the New Theatre at Richmond," and "Ode (Sung on the Occasion of Decorating the Graves of the Confederate Dead)"—written during the period of 1861–1866 in response to an emerging sense of southern nationalism. The poems, which delineate both the literal and spiritual progress of the Civil War, reflect not only the Old South's idealistic perception of its crusade but a Renaissance, particularly Shakespearian, concept of history.

The movement in Timrod's poetry to an identification with historical themes and issues is a progression characteristic of a number of nineteenth-century southern authors, such as Sidney Lanier and Mark Twain, but in Timrod's case the progression is one marked by irony. Of the writers of "the Charleston group,"[2] which included such important authors, intellectuals, and critics in the nineteenth-century South as Hugh Swinton Legare, William Gilmore Simms, Paul Hamilton Hayne, William J. Grayson, James L. Petigru, Samuel Henry Dickson, and James Matthewes Legare, Timrod was the one who most strongly advocated the belief that sectional or regional interests in literature diminished that literature's potential for universal impact and appeal. As a literary critic, Timrod saw clearly how indifferent southern culture was to the development of a significant national literature and how oppressive to native genius. In his 1859 essay, "Literature in the South," Timrod called the southern author "the Pariah of modern literature" and stated: "We think that at no time, and in no country, has the position of an author been beset with such peculiar difficulties as the Southern writer is com-

pelled to struggle with from the beginning to the end of his career."[3] With William Gilmore Simms and Paul Hamilton Hayne, two of the most prominent members of "the Charleston group," Timrod was destined throughout his career to live out the truth of Simms's dictum that "an agricultural population is rarely susceptible to the charms of art and literature."[4] Simms's and Timrod's condemnation of the South for its neglect of native talent is echoed by J. V. Ridgely in *Nineteenth-Century Southern Literature* who states that the South's "lack of concern for the professional, the inability to understand those who would make a separate career of verse-writing, was deadly to the growth of a Southern school."[5]

A deeper irony of Timrod's literary achievement resides in the fact that, despite Timrod's protestation that he regarded "the theory of Southernism in literature as a circumscription, both unnecessary and unreasonable, of the privileges of genius,"[6] Timrod is generally ranked third in order of excellence after Edgar Allan Poe and Sidney Lanier among nineteenth-century southern poets.[7] This is largely because Timrod is a singularly representative regional poet whose major work exemplifies the pastoral idealism which Lucinda Hardwick MacKethan sees as dominating nineteenth-century southern literature and giving shape and focus to modern southern literature through the works of such artists as John Crowe Ransom, Allen Tate, William Faulkner, and Robert Penn Warren.[8] In his most significant poetry Timrod expresses the theme of "the devotion to place," which Louis D. Rubin, Jr. sees as central to the matrix of Southern literature[9] and which MacKethan views as an aspect of pastoral idealism,[10] by drawing upon analogies to the Renaissance ideal in endeavoring to make a case for the south as "a special redemptive community"[11] fulfilling a significant, humanistic role in the drama of history.

Henry Timrod was born in Charleston, South Carolina, on December 8, 1828. Timrod's father, a bookbinder by trade, was also a gifted poet. Self-educated and widely read in English literature, particularly Shakespeare whom he once described as "his favorite companion,"[12] William Henry Timrod published a volume of lyric poetry in 1814 entitled *Poems on Various Sub-*

jects, one poem of which, "To Time," Washington Irving praised as equal to any lyric by Thomas Moore.[13] From his father Timrod is said to have derived an intense interest in the English classics and a deep respect for creative achievement.

Timrod received his early education at Charleston's celebrated Classical School. In 1845 he entered the University of Georgia, but sickness and limited finances forced him to withdraw without taking a degree sometime before the beginning of the August term in 1846. Returning to Charleston, he began the study of law with James L. Petigru, but quickly abandoned these studies to devote himself to literature. He became a private tutor to families in the Charleston area and began publishing verse in the *Southern Literary Messenger,* the *Southern Literary Gazette,* and various Charleston newspapers under the pseudonym "Aglaus," the name of a minor Greek poet.

During the early 1850s Timrod became friends with William Gilmore Simms and the coterie of writers and intellectuals Simms attracted. Simms's circle, which later became known as "the Charleston group," met regularly at John Russell's bookstore to discuss the arts and to foster the development of a true southern literature. To that end, the group founded *Russell's Magazine* in 1857. Paul Hamilton Hayne served as editor and Timrod as a major contributor of poems and essays. As was the usual fate with most southern periodicals, *Russell's* drew admirable reviews and much praise from its southern audience but very little financial support. In March 1860 *Russell's Magazine* published its last issue. Hayne described the venture's end in an appropriate simile: " '*Russell's,*' our small and audacious craft, which long had been sailing the ocean of literature under difficulties, chief among them the lack of golden ballast, at the close of the fourth volume struck upon breakers and sunk, like a shot, to 'Davy Jones's locker,' where she rests in peace among the fragments of a hundred similar ventures."[14]

In 1859 Timrod published his first volume of verse, *Poems,* with Ticknor & Fields of Boston. This was a work comprised primarily of pieces Timrod had earlier published in *Russell's Magazine,* the *Southern Literary Messenger,* and various Charleston newspapers. Despite Timrod's high expectations and the praise of a few reviewers, *Poems* attracted very little national attention and sold poorly. For the next few years, although he continued to contribute verse to a variety of southern periodicals, Timrod sought his living as a teacher in Bluffton, South Carolina. Roused by patriotic fervor he joined the 30th South Carolina Regiment in March 1862, but recurring bouts of tuberculosis forced his discharge from the Confederate Army on December 15, 1862.

In 1863 Timrod served as an assistant editor of the Charleston *Mercury,* and in 1864 as the associate editor of the Columbia *South Carolinian.* On February 16, 1864 he married Katie Goodwin, and on December 24, 1864 the couple's only child, Willie, was born. Shortly after his son's birth, Timrod wrote to Hayne to say that these were the happiest times of his life.[15] Timrod's joy was short-lived, however, for on February 17, 1865 Columbia was sacked and burned by Federal troops. His home and business destroyed, Timrod was forced to move his wife and son into his sister's one-story frame cottage now housing nine family members. Efforts to find new employment were unsuccessful, and Timrod's health continued to fail. On October 23, 1865, his son Willie died. In a letter to Hayne in 1866 Timrod stated: "You ask me to tell you my story for the last year. I embody it all in a few words—beggary, starvation, death, bitter grief, utter want of hope."[16]

In the final year of his life Timrod could find only sporadic employment as a clerk, a newspaper correspondent, or a tutor. Increasingly severe attacks of tuberculosis brought on violent headaches and intense hemorrhaging from the lungs. In the summer of 1867 Timrod visited Hayne in Georgia, hoping to rest and restore some of his health. In August he returned to Columbia on the promise of the editorship of a projected new daily newspaper, but when the position was actually offered late in September Timrod was too ill to accept it. He died of tuberculosis on October 7, 1867. In writing Timrod's obituary Hayne, a lifelong friend, stated that Timrod was "one of the truest and sweetest singers this country has given to the world."[17]

If Henry Timrod's literary career is prototypical of the South's neglect of its native authors, it is also representative of

the complexities inherent in nineteenth-century southern literature, as authors drawn primarily to the personal modes of artistic
expression were forced by historical circumstance to seek new
designs for the expression of ethical and societal concerns. Essentially, historicism superseded Romanticism in the nineteenth-
century South, and the artistic struggle for Timrod, as for so
many southern authors, was the development of a philosophy
which would accommodate the incorporation of historical
themes into literary expression. For Timrod the model of such a
perspective was Shakespeare, from whom Timrod derived a belief in the interrelationship of the social order and the natural
world and a sense of the fragmentation of the civilization of the
Old South as analogous to the loss of the Renaissance ideal.

Edd Winfield Parks has stated that "Timrod used Shakespeare's works freely and with evident familiarity,"[18] and the
impress of Shakespeare upon Timrod's writings can be seen
throughout his career. When Timrod endeavored to distinguish
between poetry and prose in his 1857 essay, "What is Poetry?,"
he categorized poetry as a "subtle spirit" and described prose in
lines borrowed from *Antony and Cleopatra:*

> His delights
> Were dolphin-like, they show'd his back above
> The element they liv'd in.
>
> (V.ii.88–90)[19]

When Timrod discussed the plight the southern author experienced in facing indifference from the South and hostility from
the North, he drew an analogy in the 1859 essay, "Literature in
the South," from *Henry IV, Part I:* "It would scarcely be too
absurd if we should compare his position to that of the drawer of
Shakespeare, who stands in a state of ludicrous confusion between the calls of Prince Hal upon the one side and of Poins
upon the other."[20] And in the final days of his life, when the idea
that "he was to choke to death by a sudden rush of blood from
the lungs haunted him like a spectre,"[21] two lines from *King John*
troubled him with their chilling precision: "And none of you will
bid the winter come/To thrust his icy fingers in my maw"—an

episode which Parks interprets as "graphic testimony to the power Shakespeare could wield upon Timrod's thought."[22]

While it is true that Timrod often used Shakespeare as "a source of allusions that would not require explanation,"[23] it is also apparent that Timrod envisioned Shakespeare as a mentor and that the themes, prosody, and imagery of Timrod's poetry were affected by Shakespeare's works. In *The Roots of Southern Writing,* C. Hugh Holman notes that Timrod was "well read in Elizabethan drama,"[24] while Rayburn S. Moore, in his study of Timrod's lifelong friend and poetic counterpart, Paul Hamilton Hayne, contends that Timrod acknowledged Shakespeare as a master "in the way of precept and technique."[25] Timrod himself acknowledged the indebtedness in the poem, "A Dedication," which he intended to serve as the introduction to the planned, but never completed, British edition of his poems. "A Dedication" is essentially a paean to England as a source of poetic inspiration, with Timrod stating:

> I—who, though born where not a vale
> Hath ever nursed a nightingale,
> Have fed my muse with English song
> Until her feeble wing grew strong—

and expressing his gratitude

> For many a deep and deathless lay,
> For noble lessons nobly taught,
> For tears, for laughter, and for thought,
> A portion of the mighty debt
> We owe to Shakespeare's England yet![26]

"A Dedication," which was included in Hayne's 1873 edition of Timrod's poems,[27] serves well as an introduction to a volume laced with Shakespearean influences. Some of the earliest poems included are sonnets written in direct imitation of Shakespeare and reflecting Shakespearean attitudes toward the interrelationship of love and virtue. In *Shakespeare's Sonnets: Self, Love and Art,* Philip Martin contends that a major theme of the sonnets is "the rejection of falsity, whether of heart, of speech or of appearance . . . and the praise of whatever is plain, honest, direct, natural, genuine."[28] This theme, which Martin claims identifies love with sincerity or the truth of a virtuous character,[29] is found in several of Timrod's sonnets, particularly in "Which are the Clouds" and "If I Have Graced." In these sonnets, and in several other poems centering upon love as their theme, moral beauty is seen as the transcendent quality and physical beauty as an enticing illusion of the temporal world. Frederick Turner, in *Shakespeare and the Nature of Time,* contends that "in the sonnets, as a whole, there are two great themes: love and time. Love is associated by Shakespeare with all that is warmest and most physically present in life" while time, conversely, is "the great enemy of all these beautiful and especial things; it seems to question their validity or to give a pessimistic answer to the questions they raise."[30] The onus of temporality causes Timrod, in a fashion similar to Shakespeare's, to emphasize intuition and emotion, as generators of faith, over intellect and reason, which often serve as harbingers of cynicism.[31] Aware, however, that man is a composite of both emotion and reason, passion and restraint, Timrod too envisions in his sonnets what C. H. Herford describes as Shakespeare's ideal of love—"a state in which passion and sense and intellect are united in happy balance."[32] Such sentiments in Timrod's poetry could easily be dismissed as reflections of the neoplatonic and chivalric worship of women characteristic of the nineteenth-century South were it not for the fact that Timrod in the essay, "A Theory of Poetry," cites Shakespeare as the source for his understanding of the relationship between love and truth and praises Shakespeare for the "purity, tenderness, and fidelity" of "the manner in which the element of truth appears in his descriptions of the feminine character."[33]

The most stylistically and philosophically complex of the early poems is the 558-line "A Vision of Poesy," which draws upon *A Midsummer Night's Dream* as a backdrop for its depiction of poetic inspiration as the nexus between the natural world and the mystical. The influence of Shakespeare is also apparent in the poem's prosody, for Hayne has suggested that the metrical form of "A Vision of Poesy" is that employed by Shakespeare in *Venus and Adonis.*[34]

Set "in a far country, and a distant age, /Ere sprites and fays had bade farewell to earth," "A Vision of Poesy"[35] tells of a youthful poet's quest for a mystical comprehension of the ideal through meditations upon the natural world. "One night of mist and moonlight," the poet withdraws in solitude to his favorite place in the woods, a "dark dell" encompassed by trees and covered over with wildflowers. There he falls into a dream, and a spirit appears to him. It is Poesy, "the angel of the earth," who reveals that her task is to clothe the world "with a glory all unseen" to "keep the world forever fresh and young." She tells the poet that he has been called to a "high and holy" task and urges him to be true to his mission. At this point the poet awakens from his dream. The clarity of the youth's vision has left him, and he can only cry out, "Oh! if I could tell it all, /If human speech indeed could tell it all." In the final section of the poem Poesy, as "a mystic shadow," reappears in the same "dark dell" to the poet, now in his mature years, to speak of the truths of "the inmost heart" and to reconfirm the poet in his belief that glimpses of the ideal, the ethereal, can be apprehended in the natural world.

In narrating its tale of the young poet who seeks a spiritual awareness of Nature, "A Vision of Poesy" borrows some rather obvious structural principles from *A Midsummer Night's Dream*, along with a predominant complex of images. In both works two realms or spheres exist, the real and the ethereal. The ethereal is the source of creativity and insight and is inhabited by fairies, fays, spirits, and sprites who serve as messengers of higher truths. In both "A Vision of Poesy" and *A Midsummer Night's Dream*, one enters into the ethereal realm by falling into a dream; distinctions between illusion and reality blur, and magical, wondrous things occur. Central to both works, too, is the identification of the fairy world and its mystical insights with flowers and moonlight. Ernest Schanzer, in endeavoring to account for why a play set on the eve of Mayday is called *A Midsummer Night's Dream*, states that:

> Both nights are well fitted to provide the time-setting for the supernatural events in the wood, for they are the two nights of the year when fairies were thought to be particularly powerful and when

magic and every form of witchcraft was believed to be practised. But
there are three associations which the eve of Mayday did not share
with Midsummer Night: that of flower magic, the notion being that
certain herbs and flowers gathered on that night possessed various
wonder-working powers; that of lovers' dreams; and that of
madness.[36]

In the thematic delineation of "A Vision of Poesy," Timrod, too,
attributes magical properties to flowers—properties which en-
gender dream-like trances and allow for a mystical awareness of
the ethereal realm. The "dark dell" of "A Vision of Poesy" is
covered with wildflowers which weave a "rich dais"; further, the
poet gathers flowers "inscribed with signs and characters un-
known" which serve as the "key" to opening a "wondrous mystery." Here also, as in *A Midsummer Night's Dream,* the "wondrous mystery" is revealed in a dream—an important factor, for
to Timrod "ideality and reality were not opposites" but shared a
"basic kinship" manifested in reveries and dreams.[37]

In "A Vision of Poesy," forms radiant in moonlight hold Timrod's poetic attention most strongly and spur his protagonist on
to a vision of the ideal in Nature. Among the possible concomi-
tant influences to explain this pattern of imagery, *A Midsummer
Night's Dream* seems the most logical choice, for, as Schanzer
states, in *A Midsummer Night's Dream,* "Shakespeare creates
unity of atmosphere chiefly by flooding the play with moonlight." Schanzer adds:

> There is only one daylight scene in the entire play, part of the first
> scene of Act IV, where we watch the coming of dawn and with it the
> arrival of Theseus's hunting party. And here the coming of daylight
> and the sounding of the hunting horns announce the return of sanity,
> the dispersal of magic and illusion, the end of the dream.[38]

Perhaps the most telling evidence, however, for the influence
of *A Midsummer Night's Dream* on Timrod is the progression
evident in three poems which detail essentially the same experience of a young poet's search for metaphysical insight through
communion with Nature: "The Summer Bower" (1852), "A Vision of Poesy" (1859), and "Field Flowers" (1862). In all three
poems, the poet withdraws into the woods in solitude, experi-

ences a dream-like state of reverie induced by contemplating the magical properties of flowers, and encounters a spirit which opens up to him the realm of the ethereal. In "The Summer Bower,"[39] the spiritual, creative force is called a "secret influence"; in "A Vision of Poesy," it is hailed as Poesy, "the angel of the earth" and symbol of the creative imagination; and in "Field Flowers,"[40] this spirit from the world of the divine and the ethereal is called Puck. Certainly, no more overt reference could indicate *A Midsummer Night's Dream* as the source of Timrod's inspiration than the use of Puck to represent the world of spirit, magic, and art.

The theme of the metaphysical and spiritual complexities of Nature is central to Timrod's early poetry and finds its fullest expression in "A Vision of Poesy," a work which, interestingly, is also indicative of the philosophical stances Timrod's later poetry would take. Here Poesy appears to the youthful poet to speak of the subjective ethos of lyrical Romanticism; later in the poem, Poesy reappears to tell the mature poet of his responsibility to mankind. His poetic creation is to embody truth, the spirit says, and the poet is to serve as a spokesman for the higher ideals of his community. Essentially, Poesy encourages the poet to find a sense of history—a way of envisioning and describing the historical moment as it is being shaped by the society to which the poet belongs. Thus, "the human purpose in the lay," which Poesy urges the poet to find, is the central, formative principle of Timrod's mature poetry and one which indicates a change in Timrod's perspective from the purely personal to the societal and the historical.

The perspective through which Timrod conceptualizes history in the later poems of 1860–67 is decidedly Renaissance in character. Lewis P. Simpson, in *The Dispossessed Garden: Pastoral and History in Southern Literature,* identifies the Renaissance view with what he calls the "culture of alienation," stating:

In a large sense I mean by the term that special community of discontent and disaffection formed by writers and artists in the general Western culture when, in the breaking apart of modern history, they began to experience a deficiency of wholeness, or, we may say, an incapacity to experience a cultural wholeness.[41]

In Simpson's view Shakespeare's work was one of the "first great expressions"[42] of the "culture of alienation" and Shakespeare himself was an artist with whom post-Civil War southern authors shared a measure of philosophical congruity in their perceptions of social fragmentation and the loss of a cultural ideal.

Clearly, Timrod's later poems can be associated with the "culture of alienation"—and Shakespeare's influence—in their emphasis on the theme of social fragmentation. The mature poems deal with the pathos of the human situation. Thematically, they reverse the views of the early poems, emphasizing not the beauty of man's spiritual alignment with Nature but the tragedy of man isolated from natural, cosmic, and societal harmony. In *Segments of Southern Thought,* Edd Winfield Parks claims that the course of the Civil War and the dissolution of the southern ideal can be traced in Timrod's later poetry.[43] The hopefully prophetic "The Cotton Boll" and "Ethnogenesis," the passionate "A Cry to Arms" and "Carolina," the somber "Address Delivered at the Opening of the New Theatre at Richmond," and the elegiac "Ode" to the Confederate dead represent a cosmography of a society transfigured by a sense of defeated values. The most important aspect of the later poems, to Parks, is the development of a metaphysical style, similar to that of Donne, Marvell, and Herbert, for expressing the interrelationships existing between the microcosm of the individual and society and the macrocosm of society and the natural world. In this metaphysical style Timrod makes use of complex symbols to represent the social order of the South and its unique place in history which accounts, Parks believes, for the artistic complexity and achievement of the later poems and lifts Timrod from the realm of imitator to that of visionary poet.[44]

Of the later poems written in the metaphysical style, "The Cotton Boll," "Ethnogenesis," and "Address Delivered at the Opening of the New Theatre at Richmond" are the most important, and the "Address" is the one most centered in a sense of history. Here Timrod symbolizes history as a stage upon which are enacted the various phases of southern culture, each represented by characters drawn from Shakespeare's plays. In imagery and thematic detail reminiscent of *A Midsummer Night's Dream,* the poem begins with a description of the stage as

> A fairy ring
> Drawn in the crimson of a battle plain—
> From whose weird circle every loathsome thing
>   And sight and sound of pain
> Are banished, while about it in the air,
> And from the ground, and from the low-hung skies,
>   Throng, in a vision fair
> As ever lit a prophet's dying eyes,
>   Gleams of that unseen world
> That lies about us, rainbow-tinted shapes
>   With starry wings unfurled,
> Poised for a moment of such airy capes
>   As pierce the golden foam
>   Of sunset's silent main—
> Would image what in this enchanted dome
>   Amid the night of war and death,
> In which the armed city draws its breath,
>   We have built up![45]

Within the "fairy ring" of the theatre, removed from the conflicts of the present battle, the poet states that he will reveal to his audience "souls that upon the poet's page /Have lived from age to age, /And yet have never donned this mortal clay." The poet's focus will shift from the present to the past and from life to art. Through the medium of art, he will endeavor to clarify human life. This movement from life to art he envisions as a type of transformation, "as if a desert way /Could blossom and unfold /A garden fresh with May." The present historical situation is viewed as sterile, enlivened only by art and the imagination's capacity to give meaning to events within the broader context of the relationship of the temporal moment to the timeless ideal.

In calling upon his audience to investigate and interpret the historical dimensions of southern culture, Timrod considers in the "Address" the different visions of reality represented by characters from four of Shakespeare's plays: *The Tempest, King Lear, Othello,* and *Hamlet.* Each of these characters represents a

distinct historical perspective which Timrod analyzes and compares to the present situation of his era.

The first character to appear on Timrod's imaginary stage is
Miranda of *The Tempest,* who represents an innocent view of
life, one that does not yet see the possibility of evil in human
affairs. Miranda's comment, "O brave new world" (5.1.183), is
of relevance to the Old South in the early stages of its history.
The Old South aristocrats, too, believed that they could create a
"brave new world" in human history, a dream which, as in the
"Address," the conflict of battle eventually shatters.

From Miranda's innocent view of reality in *The Tempest,* Timrod moves to a consideration of the conflict of man against nature presented in *King Lear.* Lear is "a reverend form, /With
tattered robe and forehead bare, /That challenge all the torments
of the air." He is depicted as a man contesting with the natural
universe and achieving, finally, a form of communion with it.
Both *King Lear* and *The Tempest* present images of men battling
with natural and societal forces and proving themselves equal to
both. As Timrod develops this panoply of characters for his
southern audience, he implies a direct connection between the
Shakespearean situations and conflicts and those of the audience. The South, according to Timrod, is engaged in an immense
struggle which will test the strength and nobility of all its inhabi-
tants.

The next two plays Timrod explores, *Othello* and *Hamlet,*
concern man's internal conflicts and consider in great detail
questions, of justice and the righting of wrongs. Othello and
Hamlet are both men who must struggle within themselves to
clarify their perceptions of life and to prepare themselves for its
conflicts. Hamlet embodies the characteristics which Timrod in
"Ethnogenesis" and "The Cotton Boll" attributes to the South—
he has been chosen in a corrupt world for the role of bringing
justice and creating an enduring peace in a new rule. Like the
South, Hamlet is slow to rise to the call—"He pauses on the very
brink of fact /To toy as with the shadow of an act"—but, once
challenged, he fights bravely and is willing to sacrifice his life for
the attainment of noble ideals. Timrod's use of Othello as a
character in the "Address" is of particular interest in view of the

historical context of the poem and the South's recent struggles over slavery. Certainly, the racial divisions within *Othello* and the emblematic use of black and white imagery to suggest degrees of evil and goodness would not be lost upon Timrod's audience, nor would the obvious fact that the gentle and good Desdemona, the fair symbol of virtue, is overcome and slain by the Moor. While Timrod does not elaborate on this web of associations in presenting Othello as a character, it is apparent that he could count upon his audience's familiarity with the details of Shakespeare's play and with the issues of justice, evil, and innocent suffering which the play raises to serve as a thematic and philosophical framework for the images of the South as maligned and victimized which Timrod, perhaps, wished to suggest in the "Address."

In the final section of the poem, Timrod asks if this broad range of historical vision has not found for his audience "some type to elevate a people's heart— /Some hero who shall teach a hero's part /In this distracted time." The visions which Timrod's art and imagination have presented to the South it must transform and make relevant to its own situation. With a degree of national fervor which similarly marks "Ethnogenesis," the poet expresses his belief that such heroes will arise in the South to bespeak "the whole spirit of a mighty land."

If one accepts Lewis Simpson's premise in *The Dispossessed Garden: Pastoral and History in Southern Literature* that the fracturing of the Old South ideal placed nineteenth-century southern authors in a unique position to frame an historical perspective for their society and to generate a new cultural vision,[46] it becomes apparent that artists who had earlier embraced Romantic concerns and had focused upon subjectivity as a manifestation of beauty and truth were forced by historical circumstance to seek a different, perhaps higher, vision of artistic expression. In *The Immoderate Past*, C. Hugh Holman frames the problem as the southern author's need to develop an historical imagination, one capable of envisioning "the most profound truths of the present and future in the interpretations of the past."[47]

The "Address Delivered at the Opening of the New Theatre at

Richmond" shows clearly that in the development of Timrod's historical imagination Shakespeare was his paradigm. The fictive universe Timrod hoped to create was Shakespearean—one which emphasized art's capacity to mirror and elucidate the universal truths inherent in the historical moment; one which allowed for the fusion of the personal, symbolic vision with the requirements of the ethical mode. "In this distracted time," Timrod derived from Shakespeare the capacities both to depict societal fragmentation and to reconceptualize cultural wholeness—a sequence aptly represented in the "Address" as a progression from the innocence of Miranda's vision of the world to the redeemed dignity of Hamlet's perspective of action attained through self-knowledge. The cultural wholeness Timrod seeks and projects in the "Address" is affirmative of wisdom, or the enlightenment that follows disillusionment. For the Old South, Miranda's innocence led to tragedy; Timrod suggests that from tragedy can come the regenerated spirit to believe in the brave new worlds yet to be.

Jay B. Hubbell claims that "the South has long been more conscious of its past than either the North or the West,"[48] and certainly Timrod was instrumental among the nineteenth-century Southern poets in establishing in southern literature the concept of the historical imagination—the writer's capacity to envision "the most profound truths of the present and the future in the interpretation of the past."[49] Deriving his paradigm of history from Shakespeare, Timrod was able to forge a sense of purpose and direction for his poetry and to elucidate the concerns of a society "trying under great historical stress to make an image of itself and of its meaning in history."[50] As "the Laureate of the Confederacy" and the foremost spokesman among the antebellum southern poets for "the idea that the Old South could be portrayed as a dream of Arcady,"[51] Timrod did much to establish the values of pastoral idealism as "the interior and spiritual history of the South."[52] His philosophical congruence with the Fugitive writers of the 1920s and 30s is thus strongly evident, for "the twelve southerners who wrote *I'll Take My Stand* had defended their concept of Jeffersonian agrarian innocence against the dehumanizing complexity and materialism of the urban-industrial twentieth century."[53] In much the same fashion, Timrod defended in "Ethnogenesis," "The Cotton Boll," and the "Address Delivered at the Opening of the New Theatre at Richmond" a similar ideal of pastoral innocence against the encroachment of Northern materialism and industrialization. Timrod, like the members of the Fugitive group, made a special case for the South, that "City of the Soul" which the historical Confederacy in some eyes became.[54] Robert Penn Warren, a major figure of the Fugitive era, has stated that "the Civil War is, for the American imagination, the great single event of our history" because "the Civil War is our only 'felt' history—history lived in the national imagination."[55] Clearly, Timrod contributed greatly to the sense of the Civil War as "felt history," manifesting in his major poems a cohesive vision of the emergence and loss of the Old South ideal. His unique historical imagination, Shakespearean in its composition, enabled him to view the southern experience of the Civil War as a progression from idealism to the enlightened wisdom of responsibility and to express, in terms similar to Warren's in "Last Subterfuge," the South's new vision of its destiny:

> Our grief can be endured,
> For we, at least, are men, being inured
> To wrath, to the unjust act, if need, to blood;
> And we have faith that from evil may bloom good.[56]

NOTES

1. Alfred, Lord Tennyson is reputed to have called Timrod "the Laureate of the Confederacy." Tennyson's statement is recorded in a newspaper clipping, dated New York, April 30, 1899 and signed Albert Sidney Thomas, in the Paul Hamilton Hayne Collection of the Duke University Library. The actual date of Tennyson's statement is not known. For a further discussion of this point, see *The Uncollected Poems of Henry Timrod,* ed. Guy A. Cardwell, Jr. (Athens: Univ. of Georgia Press, 1942), 2.

2. James E. Routh, Jr., in "The Poetry of Henry Timrod," *South Atlantic Quarterly* 9 (1910): 268, states that until the twentieth century America produced only two literary schools, "the New England tradition" and "the Charleston tradition"—"the Southeastern school of letters."

3. *The Essays of Henry Timrod,* ed. Edd Winfield Parks (Athens: Univ. of Georgia Press, 1942), 83. "Literature in the South" was first published in *Russell's Magazine* 5 (August 1859): 385–95.

4. William Gilmore Simms, "The Late Henry Timrod," *Southern Society* 1 (October

12, 1867): 18–19; reprinted in Jay B. Hubbell, ed., *The Last Years of Henry Timrod: 1864–1867* (Durham: Duke Univ. Press, 1942), 152–65; the quotation appears on 153–54.

5. J. V. Ridgely, *Nineteenth-Century Southern Literature* (Lexington: The Univ. Press of Kentucky, 1980), 83.

6. Timrod, *Essays,* 89.

7. Claud Green, "Henry Timrod," *Antebellum Writers in New York and the South,* vol. 3 of *Dictionary of Literary Biography* (Detroit: Gale Research Company, 1979), 339.

8. Lucinda Hardwick MacKethan, *The Dream of Arcady: Place and Time in Southern Literature* (Baton Rouge: Louisiana State Univ. Press, 1980), 1–18.

9. Louis D. Rubin, Jr., "Southern Literature and Southern Society: Notes on a Clouded Relationship," in *Southern Literary Study: Problems and Possibilities,* ed. Louis D. Rubin, Jr. and C. Hugh Holman (Chapel Hill: Univ. of North Carolina Press, 1975), 7.

10. MacKethan, 1–18.

11. Lewis P. Simpson, *The Man of Letters in New England and the South: Essays on the History of the Literary Vocation in America* (Baton Rouge: Louisiana State Univ. Press, 1973), 202.

12. Quoted in *The Poems of Henry Timrod,* ed. Paul Hamilton Hayne (New York: E. J. Hale and Son, 1873), 8–9.

13. Quoted in Ibid., 10n.

14. Paul Hamilton Hayne, "Ante-Bellum Charleston," *Southern Bivouac* 4 (November 1885): 334.

15. Quoted in *The Poems of Henry Timrod,* 44.

16. Quoted in Edd Winfield Parks, *Henry Timrod* (New York: Twayne Publishers, 1964), 44.

17. Quoted in Hubbell, 97.

18. Timrod, *Essays,* 44.

19. Ibid., 69–82; quotation appears on 76. "What is Poetry?" was originally published in *Russell's Magazine* 2 (October 1857): 52–58.

20. Timrod, *Essays,* 83.

21. Quoted in Parks, 51.

22. Timrod, *Essays,* 46; *King John* (5.8.36–37).

23. Ibid., 44.

24. C. Hugh Holman, *The Roots of Southern Writing* (Athens: Univ. of Georgia Press, 1972), 61.

25. Rayburn S. Moore, *Paul Hamilton Hayne* (New York: Twayne Publishers, 1972), 167–68.

26. *The Collected Poems of Henry Timrod,* ed. Edd Winfield Parks and Aileen Wells Parks (Athens: Univ. of Georgia Press, 1965), 17–18. "A Dedication" was first published in Hayne's edition of *The Poems of Henry Timrod,* 71.

27. Emily Timrod Goodwin, Henry Timrod's sister, wrote Hayne while he was preparing the Collected Edition (1873) that it was Timrod's wish that "A Dedication" be printed first in the order of his poems. Hayne acceded to Mrs. Goodwin's wishes; however, in the Memorial Edition of *Poems of Henry Timrod* (Boston: Houghton, Mifflin and Co., 1899)—apparently edited by W. A. Courtenay—the poem is printed fourteenth in order.

28. Philip Martin, *Shakespeare's Sonnets: Self, Love and Art* (Cambridge: Cambridge Univ. Press, 1972), 79.

29. Ibid., 79–80.

30. Frederick Turner, *Shakespeare and the Nature of Time: Moral and Philosophical Themes in Some Plays and Poems of William Shakespeare* (Oxford: Clarendon Press, 1971), 7–8.

31. Marilyn French, *Shakespeare's Division of Experience* (New York: Summit Books, 1981), 31.

32. C. H. Herford, *Shakespeare's Treatment of Love and Marriage* (1921; reprint, London: T. Fisher Unwin, Ltd., 1969), 11.

33. Timrod, *Essays,* 128. "A Theory of Poetry" was originally presented as a lecture at the Methodist Female College, Columbia, South Carolina, in the winter of 1863–64; it was not published in its entirety until 1905 when it appeared in the *Atlantic Monthly* 96 (September 1905): 313–326.

34. *The Poems of Henry Timrod,* 31.

35. Timrod, *The Collected Poems,* 63–79.

36. *A Midsummer-Night's Dream,* in *Shakespeare: The Comedies,* ed. Kenneth Muir (Englewood Cliffs: Prentice-Hall, 1965), 27.

37. Edd Winfield Parks, "Timrod's Concept of Dreams," *South Atlantic Quarterly* 48 (October 1949): 585.

38. Schanzer, 29.

39. Timrod, *The Collected Poems,* 26–28.

40. Timrod, *The Uncollected Poems,* 99–102.

41. Lewis P. Simpson, *The Dispossessed Garden: Pastoral and History in Southern Literature* (Athens: Univ. of Georgia Press, 1975), p. 34.

42. Ibid., 34.

43. Edd Winfield Parks, *Segments of Southern Thought* (Athens: Univ. of Georgia Press, 1938), 102.

44. Timrod, *Essays,* 46.

45. Timrod, *The Collected Poems,* 119–122.

46. Simpson, *The Dispossessed Garden,* 65–100.

47. C. Hugh Holman, *The Immoderate Past: The Southern Writer and History* (Athens: Univ. of Georgia Press, 1977), 1.

48. Jay B. Hubbell, *Southern Life in Fiction* (Athens: Univ. of Georgia Press, 1960), 11.

49. Holman, *The Immoderate Past,* 1.

50. Lewis P. Simpson, "The South's Reaction to Modernism: A Problem in the Study of Southern Letters," in Rubin and Holman, 62.

51. MacKethan, 3.

52. Simpson, *The Man of Letters,* 218.

53. F. Garvin Davenport, Jr., *The Myth of Southern History: Historical Consciousness in Twentieth-Century Literature* (Nashville: Vanderbilt Univ. Press, 1970), 131.

54. Paul West, "Robert Penn Warren," in *American Writers: A Collection of Literary Biographies,* ed. Leonard Unger, vol. 4 (New York: Scribner's, 1974), 238.

55. *The Legacy of the Civil War: Meditations on the Centennial* (New York: Random House, 1961), 3–4.

56. Robert Penn Warren, "Last Subterfuge," in *Selected Poems: 1923–1975* (New York: Random House, 1976), 39–40.

Lanier and Shakespeare

Thomas Daniel Young

During the last few years of his relatively short life, while he was occupying the chair of first flutist in the Baltimore Symphony Orchestra, Sidney Lanier gave a series of public lectures at the Peabody Institute and Johns Hopkins University on the development of English literature, some of which were devoted to Shakespeare and his time. These lectures were published twenty-five years after Lanier's death as *Shakspere and His Forerunners: Studies in Elizabethan Poetry* (1902). Although Lanier was genuinely interested in the development of English poetry, his comments on Shakespeare reveal that he was indeed a true child of his age. The plays he liked best were those in which he thought he could find "an uplifting moral." A born musician with an undeniable interest in and talent for music, Lanier was apparently more attracted to the sonnets than to the plays. Although he planned to center his lectures to the Peabody Institute (1878–79) on Shakespeare's poetry, the lectures finally given present Shakespeare in terms of his setting and stem in part from Lanier's conviction that Shakespeare came out of the Anglo-Saxon tradition and that his works mark the climax of English literature.

Trying to establish firmly in the minds of his audience the tradition that bred Shakespeare as its finest writer, Lanier confined the first twenty-four of his lectures to the writers from Beowulf to Chaucer and his contemporaries. Even the lectures advertised as his "Shakspere Course" ranged broadly over the late sixteenth and early seventeenth centuries and made few specific comments on Shakespeare's poetry: one lecture was devoted to the development of the language from Chaucer to Shakespeare; five discussed the development of the sonnet from Surrey through Milton (only one of these concentrated on Shakespeare's contributions to the form); two were announced

to be on pronunciation in Shakespeare's time, but one was devoted to drama as sermon and the other comments on some
fairly obvious instances that appear to be false rhyme but are
merely changes in pronunciation that have occurred since
Shakespeare's time.[1] To the student of Shakespeare the two
most helpful lectures of the series are on Renaissance music.
The course concluded with four lectures on domestic life in
Shakespeare's time, the last two of which were organized
around an imaginary life of Shakespeare—his education, his
home life, the places he visited, and the means of entertainment
(including the drama) available to him.

Although the lectures are filled with errors, Kemp Malone has
indicated that they seem "to reflect fairly accurately" the best
scholarship available to Lanier (p. xix). In many instances the
lectures reveal that Lanier merely represented the interests and
convictions of his age—the tireless search through the plays for
"uplifting morals" and the unshakable faith in the doctrine of
progress, for instance. Many of the lectures demonstrate, however, that he was reaching beyond the limits of his time. The
discussions of "Shakspere's forerunners" offer convincing evidence of Lanier's interest in and knowledge of the English literary tradition. He handled with ease and often with surprising
penetration the little-known works of Thomas Wyatt, John Lyly,
Phineas Fletcher, and Samuel Daniel, and he always insisted that
these writers deserved more attention than they had received. In
fact, he informed his audience, "after you have read the Bible
and Shakspere, you have no time to read anything else until you
have read these."

The basic thrust of the lectures apparently was to show Shakespeare as hero, humankind at the height of its development—
surely an ambitious and worthy endeavor, which Lanier was
always promising to undertake but never quite succeeded in
tackling. Instead his approach to the few plays that he discussed
was oblique and eccentric. His lectures say little about Shakespeare's art. *Hamlet,* according to Lanier, reveals man's increasing knowledge of the supernatural: Hamlet does not murder
Claudius while he is praying because he thinks that Claudius's
soul will go to heaven as a result. Lanier's conception of Hamlet

is that he "does not believe in heaven or hell: he makes heaven and hell mere excuses for irresolution. He is a weak, unnerved, good man, who would be strong if he had faith of any sort" (16). That Lanier had read Coleridge and did not fully understand or agree with him is obvious. Similarly Lanier holds that *Beowulf* and *A Midsummer Night's Dream* illustrate man's changing attitude toward nature. In *Beowulf* nature is represented as "crackling chasms in the solid earth," "convulsions of quaking continents and pouring seas." In every scene in the poem nature is presented as having a "grim, inexorable savagery" (27). Thinking, no doubt, of the Romantic attitude toward nature, Lanier insists that "today the mood of nature is finer and sweeter" and "reveals itself in unspeakable beauty" (27). In *Beowulf* nature is still in her savage mood; her clear intent is to harm man, if not to destroy him. In *A Midsummer's Night's Dream,* however, all restraints between man and nature are broken down. Man communes with nature freely. No longer is it necessary to struggle in order to conquer the wild spirit of nature; now man needs only to demonstrate his love of the natural world. (36)

In the lectures on "Pronunciation in Shakspere's Time" the emphasis is not only on the difficulties the modern reader has with Shakespeare's rhyme but also on Lanier's theory that the characters in Shakespeare's plays do not speak as men or women would in real life; their speeches, instead, are intended "to give a true conception of the emotions that underlie them" (190). Moral teachings are clear and compelling in the plays because there is no "glazing and covering over of crimes as there is in real life. . . . The play of Shakspere can teach us a clear lesson, can preach us a clear sermon where the deliverance of real life is uncertain and confused" (192). Lanier interprets the *Two Gentlemen of Verona,* for example, as a sermon on "constancy of love and friendship." It demonstrates "the beauty of constancy," "the ugliness of treachery," and the "grandeur of that forgiveness which pardons the trespasser in these matters . . . involving human happiness." Likewise, he says, *Cymbeline, The Tempest,* and *The Winter's Tale* "all present the importance and necessity of true forgiveness."

Shakespeare's sonnets, Lanier insists, present the figure of a lover quite different from that in earlier English sonnets. He refers specifically to those sonnets dedicated to the "man he loves." To Lanier, Shakespeare's sonnet sequence to the young man details the "progress of a friendship between two men." The man betrayed Shakespeare and took advantage of their friendship to steal the affections of the woman Shakespeare loved; nevertheless, Shakespeare forgave him, even invented excuses for his friend's "perfidious act."

The sonnet beginning "Shall I compare you to a summer's day?" not only indicates Shakespeare's adoration of his friend but also his loneliness in his absence. Other sonnets demonstrate other aspects of Shakespeare's affection. In sonnet 43, Lanier insists—in a statement that sounds very similar to some of the arguments of many twentieth-century critics, although toward very different ends—that "this poem, instead of being inspired by manly friendship" seems to have been "penned by some woman's lover in a moment of estatic adoration" (159). The poem is structured, Lanier perceptively observes, so that by using a term in a double sense, "the poet causes significations to meet in the same word, like two lips kissing out a new meaning." He offers an example to prove his contention:

> When most I wink, then do my eyes best see,
> For all the day they view things unrespected;
> But when I sleep, in dreams they look on thee,
> And, darkly bright are bright in dark directed;
> . . . .
> All days are nights to see, still I see thee,
> And nights, bright days, when dreams do show thee me.

After this discussion Lanier draws his inevitable moral: the world at large was as ignorant of Shakespeare's greatness as his friend was. Lanier observes that he was little known by the person whom Shakespeare regarded as the man of men. The greatest poet in the language is likened by Lanier unto the mountain, of which one cannot perceive its true worth until he is removed a certain distance from it. The sonnet sequence clearly reveals, Lanier concludes, that "even his one friend and his one love, after all the intimacy of their relations, so faintly saw his greatness that he took from the poet the single comfort of his life" (167). Surely Lanier would be shocked and upset if he were aware of the meaning some present-day readers would attach to this statement.

Of the sixteen lectures Lanier gave at Johns Hopkins on "English Verse" (especially Shakespeare) during 1879–80, only five complete lectures and parts of two others survive. After an introductory lecture stating the theme and the proposed subjects of the series, Lanier divides the plays into what he calls the "Bright Period—1590–1601," which includes most of the comedies and histories; the "Dark Period—1601–1608," the tragedies; and the "Heavenly Period—1608–1613," the "Plays of Forgiveness." The chief burden of the subsequent lectures is to justify and explain the reasons for this division. Using such terms as "metrical tests," "Rime," "Run-on and End-Stopped Lines," "Man's Relation to God," "Man's Relations to Man," and "Relations of Man to Nature," Lanier examines one play from each period—usually *A Midsummer Night's Dream, Hamlet,* and *The Tempest*—to trace Shakespeare's intellectual and spiritual development.

Lanier's introductory lecture is intended to remind his audience of the importance of poetry, which "comes from above and preaches its gospel to men." It "has created an ideal world in which we moderns move and live and have our being" (312). Poetry has created the world man lives in; we are "completely and practically the creatures of English literature." Such poets as Chaucer and Shakespeare, Lanier tells his audience, "moulded the very soul of your ancestors before you" (313). Literature has translated the Bible, created and shaped the Constitution, the social codes, the systems of private morals. No one can escape the influence of literature, for like Emerson's Brahma it is "the wings wherewith we fly." Poetry is the only art which does not require technical knowledge, Lanier continues; it is readily available to all. Any poet, furthermore, can justify anything he does by referring to Chaucer or Shakespeare. Bad criticism has not been able to affect Shakespeare's reputation for three hundred years because he was the supreme master in the use of verse forms and because he possessed "moral superiority." Finally, Lanier pays the poet the supreme compliment, saying he is "the maker presiding at the genesis of a poem like the Creator presiding at the genesis of the world" (317).

Shakespeare's inward development is revealed, Lanier argues, as we review the plays that fall into each of the three divisions that he has devised. Shakespeare's attitudes, feelings, and temperament during a particular period are revealed in the plays he wrote during that time. The plays of the first period, Lanier holds, reveal a vivacious imagination, a youth "rioting about the contemporary scene and down through the ages like a young swallow in the early morning, now flitting his wings in the water—and like as not dirty water—now sailing over the meadow grass, now sweeping through the upper heights of heaven" (330). All the comedies, Lanier notes, belong to this period: *Love's Labor's Lost, Two Gentlemen of Verona, A Midsummer Night's Dream, The Merchant of Venice, As You Like It, Twelfth Night.* The works of this period include but one tragedy, *Romeo and Juliet,* and the real thrust of that play is not the tragic death of the two young lovers but their young love, "which is depicted with the unspeakable fire and the freshness of a young imagination" (330). The play is really a "bridegroom's passionate song set off with the funeral hymn for a foil."

Even the history plays, according to Lanier, seem to be "written from without." They do not center around one crime of passion, as the tragedies do; their manner is lighter and more personal than that characterizing the period of *Hamlet, Macbeth, Othello,* and *King Lear.* The history plays reflect the manner of a young man, one "who has not yet been brought into any actual conflict and dreadful grind with the forces of nature and of accident and passion and of the twist of life in his own personal relations with his fellowman" (331). In *Henry VI* and *Richard III,* says Lanier, Shakespeare is writing under the influence of Marlowe, and in *Richard II* and *King John* he is trying to convert weak men into strong kings. To perform this feat he has to rely heavily on his fertile imagination and his as yet unabated optimism. In *Henry IV* he is writing a showpiece for Falstaff and disregarding historical fact almost entirely. These two plays, *Henry IV, Parts I and II,* should be regarded as comedies, not histories. Although *Henry V* is in a more serious vein, Shakespeare is more concerned here, Lanier contends, with the transformation of the character of young Prince Hal when he learns of his father's death than he is with relaying historical fact. It is obvious, however, Lanier continues, that about the time he wrote *Henry V* something was thrusting him into a more serious vein, something very terrible "profoundly shaking his heart."

Although there had been personal tragedies in Shakespeare's life before now—such as his father's business failure and the death of his son—he continued to write light comedy. But now, about 1600 or a little later, Lanier says, there was a "tremendous wrench of his soul." Something happened, Lanier insists, because after a series of light comedies, ending with *Twelfth Night,* there came a series of bloody tragedies, beginning with *Julius Caesar* and *Hamlet* and followed by *Measure for Measure,* that "wretched slough of a play . . . all murky with shame and weakness and brutality and low suffering and death and dark questions." Soon thereafter came "the enormous single-passion tragedies": *Othello, King Lear, Macbeth, Anthony and Cleopatra, Coriolanus,* and *Timon of Athens.* Lanier finds evidence of this change in some of the sonnets, from LXVI to CXII. For example:

> No longer mourn for me when I am dead
> Than you shall hear the surly sullen bell
> Give warning to the world that I am fled
> From this vile world with vilest worms to dwell.
> (LXXI)
> O, lest the world should task you to recite
> What merit liv'd in me, that you should love
> After my death, dear love, forget me quite,
> For you in me can nothing worthy prove;
> Unless you would devise some virtuous lie.
> (LXXII)
> Then hate me when you wilt, if ever, now,
> Now while the world is bent my deeds to cross,
> Join with the spite of fortune, make me bow,
> And do not drop in for an after-loss.

Ah, do not, when my heart hath 'scaped this sorrow,
Come in the rearward of a conquer'd woe;
(XC)

As suddenly as Shakespeare entered this period of dark despair, Lanier says, he came out of it and moved into "The Heavenly Period" (334). His moods were now marked by a calm optimism as if he had "attained God out of knowledge and good out of a infinite pain." The plays written during this period—*Pericles, Cymbeline, The Tempest, The Winter's Tale, Henry VIII*—are "in great and noble music, breathe of new love after estrangement, or recovery of long-lost children, of the kissing of wives thought dead, of reconciliation, of new births of old happiness." Lanier concludes, therefore, that these plays were written in a period of calm initiated by assured victory. About 1612 Shakespeare went back to Stratford, Lanier speculates, to reconcile his differences with his wife and there live the life of a simple citizen with "wife, children, grandchild and friends."

Lanier dates the plays according to the following systems: "the Rime test, the Run-on and End-stopped line test, the Weak-ending test, the Double-ending test and the Rhythmic Accent test." He concludes that the plays with the highest percentage of rhymes were written in the first period; those with the lowest in the last. The plays with the largest percentage of run-on lines belong to the last period; those with the highest percentage of end-stopped lines were written in the first period. "The versification of the late plays," Lanier argues, "is freer, more natural, and larger in music than that of the earlier plays," and the use of run-on lines gives "a certain advance in breadth of view which simply embodies in technic that spiritual advance in majesty of thought, in elevation of tone, in magnanimity, in largeness of moral scope." He continues, resorting again to musical comparisons to make his point:

Those of you who heard the Romance in the *Suite* by Bach played at the Peabody concerts last winter will remember the sense of heavenly breadth and infinite expanse given by the length of the musical phrases which Bach has there employed; and if you compare the grandeur of these phrases with the slighter proportioned phrases of an ordinary waltz or march, you will have a good musical analogue of the difference between Shakspere's later verse, which is full of run-on lines and his earlier ones, which is full of end-stopped ones; while at the same time you will have a good musical analogue of the difference between the moral width and nobleness of such plays as *The Winter's Tale* and *The Tempest* and all this forgiveness-and-reconcilliation group and the wild, delicious riot and unabating abandon of the comedy group. (342)

Lanier then turns to the weak-ending lines (ones ending in "some merely connective word," a preposition, conjunction, or auxiliary verb). These weak endings serve a relational function, he argues; the meaning of a line ended in this fashion is incomplete without the next line. Light-ending words are such as *be, am, could,* and any auxiliary verb or pronoun. A weak ending is one of the still less important words, such as *and, if, or, but,* or *so. After an exacting count Lanier concludes that Shakespeare's use of weak- or light-ending lines began abruptly with Macbeth.* There is not a single weak-ending line in *Two Gentlemen,* only one in *A Midsummer Night's Dream,* two in *As You Like It,* in *Twelfth Night,* four; in *Macbeth,* twenty-three; in *Antony and Cleopatra,* ninety-nine.

It is clear, Lanier is convinced, that Shakespeare changed his theory of versification. Since the run-on line gave him more freedom of expression, he discovered the weak- or light-ending line—a kind of run-on line that compels the reader to move without hesitation on to the next line—and found it particularly appealing.

The double-ending line Lanier compares to a bar of music in which the last quarter note is "split into its two equivalent eighth notes, and the bar has three sounds instead of two." In poetry the double-ending line may conclude with one word such as "vessel" or two, as "in her." Like the disuse of rhyme, the run-on line, or the weak-ending line, the double-ending line is a "variation of the normal form," a departure from regimented structural firmness.

All three of these variations from regular structure are used much more frequently in the later plays than in the earlier. Lanier notes, too, that this loosening up of structural demands became characteristic of Shakespeare's later style so that we can determine with great precision which parts of *Henry VIII* were written by Shakespeare and which by Fletcher. In a similar manner application of these metrical tests demonstrate that Shakespeare and Fletcher wrote *The Two Noble Kinsmen;* we also know every passage that Shakespeare wrote and every one Fletcher wrote.

Lanier summarizes his findings on Shakespeare's versification in these major points: Shakespeare tended as his career progressed to disuse rhyme; his later verse has fewer end-stopped lines than the earlier; there is a similar increase in weak-ending lines in the later poetry; the later plays include many more examples of double-ending lines; with all of these tactics, as in the changes of normal rhythmic accents, Shakespeare was striving for more freedom, trying to make his verse less monotonous, and searching for more individuality. Lanier is careful to note, however, that Shakespeare's attempts to gain more freedom are not frenzied or chaotic but carefully and artistically controlled. Even in his later plays he used some rhyme and employed some end-stopped lines. The normal ending of his line was strong not weak, single-ending not double, and the greater number of his rhythmic accents were in the normal or expected places. His advance toward freedom was temperate, always respecting the regularity of verse structure. What Shakespeare attempted to do, as he mastered his art, was to balance artistically the oppositions of which verse is made.

One wonders what to say about these particular lectures. Surely they are not reliable scholarship and one learns little about Shakespeare from them. It seems evident, however, that Lanier read widely in English literature from the Anglo-Saxons through the Elizabethans and that he was just as knowledgeable about British history, including social and economic developments. There are, of course, many places at which the modern reader would disagree with Lanier's reading of Shakespeare. A child of his age, Lanier searched constantly for an "uplifting moral." As John Crowe Ransom once said of himself, Lanier was certainly a "homemade scholar," but he had an amazing grasp of much of the extant scholarship in language and phonetics, and much of this scholarship he summarized for his audience of laymen so that they could understand it. His philological studies made him particularly enthusiastic about Old and Middle English literature, and this love of our earliest writers he passed on not only to his lecture audiences but even to modern readers whom the essays continue to stimulate even when they mystify. Much of the Anglo-Saxon poetry he read to his audience he had to render into modern English, and some of these translations are still impressive today. Much of his scholarly study went into metrics, and although some of his findings made their way into *Shakspere and His Forerunners,* most of them went into *The Science of English Verse.* As Kemp Malone has pointed out, "Lanier entered academic scholarship a well-read man, at home in the world of literature, already a true philologist in the old sense of that word; that is, a lover of literary learning."

Most modern readers—who feel that the primary purpose of literature is to help one to "realize" the world, not to "idealize" it—cannot forgive Lanier for insisting constantly that "all things work for the good of man." At the highest level, he insisted, "poetry makes good of ill." Consequently, what one can make of the lectures on Shakespeare's life and the effect of his personal life upon the poetry is difficult to determine. In the first place Lanier admitted that in the fourth quarter of the nineteenth century little was known of Shakespeare's personal life. Lanier proposed to create "a romance . . . in which taking Shakspere for a hero I propose to weave a picture of the manners of his contemporaries" (249). What emerges in the lectures generally does not contradict what we know of life in sixteenth-century England, and the experiences he creates *could* have happened to Shakespeare. The lectures make good reading and they must have enhanced his audience's appreciation for Shakespeare. The events he describes are not based on fact, and the effect of these events on the plays is pure speculation, but Lanier does not claim otherwise. Finally, one suspects the most important contribution of these lectures to Shakespeare criticism is that they reveal Lanier's deep and genuine appreciation of Shakespeare and that his love for the master was infectious. He passed it on to all who listened to the lectures and to those today who read *Shakspere and His Forerunners* and *The Science of English Verse.*

NOTE

1. Material for this paper came from the following sources: *Shakspere and His Forerunners,* ed. Kemp Malone, vol. 3 of *The Centennial Edition of the Works of Sidney Lanier,* Charles R. Anderson, gen. ed., 10 vols. Baltimore: Johns Hopkins Press, 1945 p. viii. Hereafter referred to by page number in the text. Also, *The Science of English Verse,* vol. 2 of the above.

Is Shakespeare Dead?
Mark Twain's Irreverent Question

Thomas J. Richardson

Alan Gribben's recent reconstruction of Mark Twain's library documents the breadth and depth of Twain's reading, including an amazing amount of Shakespeare.[1] Twain's public posture during his later years (one supported by William Dean Howells)—that he was an "unliterary literary man," ignorant of tradition—was, of course, contrived, as a number of scholars have pointed out.[2] Gribben and John Baetzhold define and annotate a remarkable range of Shakespearean allusions, influences, puns, and quotations in Twain's work.[3] With their work as a guide, a reading of Twain's canon, including the now published papers, notebooks, and journals, reveals that Twain knew his Shakespeare very well indeed. Gribben lists extensive citations from Twain's work alluding to twenty-five plays, especially *Hamlet*, to *Venus and Adonis,* and to Sonnet 144. In addition, he establishes that Twain's library held a variety of single and multivolume Shakespearean editions, as well as the Lippincott *Mottoes and Aphorisms from Shakespeare.* Twain read Shakespeare frequently throughout his career, and his earliest works show evidence of such reading.[4]

Indeed, Walter Blair speculates that Twain knew Shakespeare well enough to compose the Duke's famous garbled Shakespearean soliloquy in *Adventures of Huckleberry Finn* (1885) "from memory," although there has been further discussion of the text's genesis.[5] Certainly Twain had heard and seen Shakespeare's plays as well as read them. In the "Old Times" section of *Life on the Mississippi* (1883) and later in *Is Shakespeare Dead?* (1909), Twain comments on his relationship with George Ealer, one of the pilots on the steamboat *Pennsylvania.* Twain says that Ealer was "an idolator of Shakespeare" who "—quite uninvited—would read Shakespeare to me; not just casually, but

by the hour, when it was his watch and I was steering. He read well, but not profitably for me, because he constantly injected commands into the text."[6] In *Is Shakespeare Dead?* Twain recalls Ealer's reading from *Macbeth:*

What man dare, I dare!
Approach thou *what* are you laying in the leads for? What a hell of an idea! like the rugged ease her off a little, ease her off! rugged Russian bear, the armed rhinoceros or the *there* she goes! meet her, meet her! didn't you *know* she'd smell the reef if you crowded it like that? Hyrcan tiger; take any shape but that and my firm nerves she'll be in the *woods* the first you know! stop the starboard!
Come ahead strong on the larboard! back the starboard! . . . *Now* then, you're all right; come ahead on the starboard; straighten up and go 'long, never tremble: or be alive again, and dare me to the desert *damnation* can't you keep away from that greasy water? pull her down! snatch her! snatch her baldheaded! With thy sword; if trembling I inhabit then, lay in the leads!—no, only the starboard one, leave the other alone, protest me the baby of a girl. Hence horrible shadow! eight bells—that watchman's asleep again, I reckon, go down and call Brown yourself, unreal mockery, hence!

Ealer's treatment of Shakespeare was, perhaps, good preparation for the Duke's pastiche, and as Baetzhold notes Ealer probably "sparked the real development of [Twain's] affection for Shakespeare's works."[7] However, Twain saw a wide variety of more legitimate Shakespeare productions during his lifetime, among them Forrest's *Othello* and Booth's *Hamlet.* His early theater experiences included a "river-town rendition of *Richard III*" and a professional *Julius Caesar* in St. Louis.[8] During his newspaper days in Nevada and California, he reviewed a number of "gold coast" theater productions, especially in San Francisco where the theater had achieved excellence during the 1850s.[9] He was, as Sydney Krause says, a "lifelong theatergoer";[10] for example, the notebooks reveal that he saw *Lear* at Mannheim (1877), that he attended the Shakespeare festival in Cincinnati (1883), and that he saw *Othello* at the Metropolitan (1885), among many other productions.[11] He also bought copies of Shakespeare for amateur productions; Clara Clemens remembers parlor performances of *Hamlet* (1881) and *Macbeth* (1885).[12]

With such acquaintance as a context, it was natural that Twain's works should draw directly on Shakespeare in a variety of ways, both major and minor. Neither Gribben's extensive list of allusions nor Baetzhold's commentary need be duplicated here; as Baetzhold says, Twain "levied frequently on Shakespeare to make a point or enhance a description."[13] It does not seem necessary, either, to catalogue all of Twain's "major" uses of Shakespeare, such as the well-known parallel between *Romeo and Juliet* and the Shepherdson–Grangerford feud in *Huckleberry Finn*, the parallels between the Henry plays and *Joan of Arc* (1896), the use of Shakespeare as a character in the ribald *1601, Conversation As it was by the Social Fireside in the Time of the Tudors* (1876), the Shakespearean influences in the maxims of Pudd'nhead Wilson's calendar, or the influence of Shakespeare's language and plot devices on *The Prince and the Pauper* (1882). What I will attempt, instead, is a brief survey of four "representative" texts—beginning with the early newspaper piece, "The Killing of Julius Caesar Localized" (1864), along with Twain's unfinished burlesque of *Hamlet* (1881), the Duke's speech in *Huckleberry Finn* (1885), and *Is Shakespeare Dead?* (1909), an essay treating the Shakespeare–Bacon controversy. These four texts provide a survey of Twain's prevailing interest in Shakespeare, early and late; perhaps more important, they offer some general sense of Twain's ambivalent attitude toward Shakespeare and his works, as part of his characteristic ambivalence toward established civilization, traditional standards, and classic literature.

That Twain admired Shakespeare's work is certain, as his continual reading and a host of his allusions demonstrate. In a notebook entry (Monday, January 7, 1889, 4:45 p.m.), regarding his new Paige typesetter, Twain says that "the first proper name ever set by this new keyboard was William Shakspere." Yet his basic approach is irreverent, leaning toward the burlesque, with humor springing from the incongruity between Shakespeare's language, characters, and plots on the one hand, and Twain's contemporary society on the other. As a result, both worlds are deflated, laughed at, and criticized. The contrived posture that Twain nurtured—of being an "unliterary literary man"—reveals something of his antagonism toward the civilized world, even toward its classic literature. The ambivalence and tensions evident in the Whittier birthday speech (and Twain's chagrin over it)—irreverence vs. admiration—are also visible in these four pieces on Shakespeare. In *1601,* the Queen's cupbearer (the Mark Twain of his day) listens to Shakespeare read part of *Henry IV* to the assembled fireside guests, and concludes it has not the value of an "arsefull of ashes." Shakespeare then reads a portion of *Venus and Adonis,* which the cupbearer "did deme . . . but paltry stuff."[14] Finally, as *Is Shakespeare Dead?* discloses, Twain at last came to regard Shakespeare the man as a "claimant," much in the mold of Twain's other false claimants, to fame, fortune, and power. In fact, this point is made as early as 1873, during Twain's visit to Stratford. Among the notebook comments about Stratford as in institution, Twain is already saying that the lack of biographical information about Shakespeare is "quite remarkable."[15]

Among his apprentice writings, Twain published three lectures in the Keokuk *Post* during 1856–57 under the name Thomas Jefferson Snodgrass; the first of these (October 18, 1856), apparently written after he saw *Julius Caesar* in St. Louis, presents an illiterate country bumpkin burlesquing the play. Though he soon abandoned Thomas Jefferson Snodgrass for the more erudite Shakespeare-quoting Quintius Curtius Snodgrass in ten letters for the New Orleans *Crescent* (January 21–March 30, 1861), Twain returned to *Julius Caesar* for his first extended use of Shakespeare, "The Killing of Julius Caesar Localized," in the *Californian,* November 12, 1864.[16] Baetzhold describes this as "a more skillful burlesque than has generally been noted," and notes that its humor comes not only from "the sometimes ludicrous clash of the narrator's modern idiom with the readers' memories of Shakespeare," but also from its satire of contemporary journalism.[17] As "the only true and reliable account" of Caesar's murder, this piece offers a translation from a fictional Roman newspaper, "The Daily Evening Fasces." The "local" San Francisco report is made fun of here, with its cliches of treating a violent murder and its aftermath. E. M. Branch and Robert Hirst suggest that Clemens strikes blows here not only at journalistic "localizing" but also "at the social and political mores of San Francisco," where murder has become an "item."[18] Here a reporter "takes a living delight" in "gathering up the details of a bloody and mysterious murder, and writing them up with aggravated circumstantiality." If possible, Twain's reporter could scoop the other papers by arriving "at the base of Pompey's statue in time to say persuasively to the dying Caesar: 'O, come now, you ain't so far gone, you know, but what you could stir yourself up a little and tell a fellow just how this thing happened, if you was a mind to, couldn't you—now do!' and get the 'straight of it' from his own lips."

The "translation" is based on act 3, especially, of *Julius Caesar,* but here classic tragedy is reduced to an "election row." Rome, according to Twain's reporter, has "never even been able to choose a dog-pelter without celebrating the event with a dozen knock-downs and a general cramming of the station-house with drunken vagabonds overnight." Mr. George W. Cassius (the "Nobby boy of the Third Ward") is "a bruiser in the pay of the opposition." The reporter describes how, while Mr. J. Caesar "was talking to some of the back-country members about the approaching fall elections," Billy Trebonius, Casca, Brutus, and others attack. Caesar "launches a blow" at Casca that sends "the reptile bleeding to the earth." At the same time senators were "flying down the aisles in wild confusion toward the shelter of the committee-rooms, and a thousand voices were shouting 'PO-LICE! PO-LICE!' " Caesar's coat, "found to be cut and gashed in no less than seven different places. . . . will be exhibited at the coroner's request, and will be damning proof of the fact of the killing." The report concludes by noting that as "we go to press, the Chief of Police is satisfied there is going to be a riot, and is taking measures accordingly." "The Killing of Julius Caesar Localized" is an apprentice piece, somewhat strained in places, but Twain did not hesitate even this early in his career to burlesque Shakespeare. Indeed, as noted, the humor of Twain's text depends on our memory of Shakespeare's play. High tragedy and Latin names are set in a contemporary, vernacular context, and our laughter cuts both ways. The strongest criticism here may be of modern San Francisco journalism, but Shakespeare is deflated as well.

Hamlet was one of Twain's perennial favorites, as Gribben's extensive list of allusions demonstrates. An idea which persisted with him was a burlesqued *Hamlet*,[19] with the addition of a contemporary character much like Hank Morgan in the anachronistic setting of Malory's Camelot. He apparently proposed the addition of such a character for humorous modern comment to Edwin Booth in a backstage conversation in 1873. Booth "laughed immoderately," according to Orion Clemens. Walter Blair says that "immoderately" should probably be read "hysterically."[20] At any rate Twain burned his early version of the burlesque, as he notes in an 1881 letter to Howells, mainly—and curiously—because he had been reluctant to make violent alterations in Shakespeare's original text. But he began once more:

> At your house . . . an old idea came again into my head . . . that of adding a character to *Hamlet*. I did the thing once—nine years ago; the addition was a country cousin of Hamlet's. But it did not suit me, and I burnt it. A cousin wouldn't answer; the family could not consistently ignore him; one couldn't rationally explain a *cousin's* standing around the stage during 5 acts and never being spoken to; for the sacrilegious scribbler who ventured to put words into Shakespeare's mouth would probably be hanged. But I've got a character, now, who is all right. He goes and comes as he pleases; yet he does not need to be spoken to. I've done the first and second Acts; but this was too much work for three days.[21]

Twain did not complete or publish this 1881 burlesque, but the fragment which survives (through act 2, scene 2) is a significant record of his project. In 1879 he had written in his notebook, "Try Hamlet again, and make free with Shakspere—let Hamlet and everybody else talk with the fellow. . . ."[22] Yet, as the Howells letter indicates, while Twain's new character "goes and comes as he pleases . . . he does not need to be spoken to." His correspondence with Joseph T. Goodwin (Twain's former editor at the Virginia City *Enterprise*) reveals that Twain's choice for the new character, a foster brother, had been made prior to the burst of creative activity on the burlesque in 1881. In the existing

play, the foster brother, Basil Stockmar, is also a traveling book
agent. Twain was encouraged in the *Hamlet* project by his
friends, especially Howells and Goodwin. In fact, when Twain
abandoned the project, Goodwin apparently sent him a completed manuscript of his own based on the blood brother idea,
asking Twain's collaboration. Twain did not respond, and Franklin Rogers speculates that "a possible reason for the cool reception of Goodwin's effort" might be found in Goodwin's cover
letter: "I was speaking to Burnett once about your idea, and he
thought it would be a sort of sacrilege." While Goodwin scoffed
at the "sacrilege" idea, "he may have evoked unwittingly those
scruples" which Twain had evidenced before.[23] Should he really
"make free with Shakespeare?" Should he violate so sacred a
text?

Twain's approach in "The Death of Julius Caesar Localized"
was less direct and perhaps did not raise these difficult questions, for that burlesque of Shakespeare's play was relatively
mild. In an interesting note, Rogers says, "I must confess my
inability to understand Twain's scruples. Apparently Twain did
not object to a disruption of the total fabric of *Hamlet* with the
introduction of a new character, but he did object violently to the
disruption or alteration of individual speeches or lines. The effects of the scruples are easily perceived, but the scale of values
behind them defies analysis."[24] Here again is evidence of Twain's
ambivalence toward his subject, a model acknowledged as the
greatest writer in English literature. Twain's scale of values does
indeed defy analysis, though his divided sensibility and its impact on his life and work have often been discussed. Twain's
wish to be part of the great tradition and the society from which
it sprang, set against his criticism of its faults, could produce a
powerful tension in his great works; at the same time he could be
(and has been) accused of confusion and lack of coherence.

In the existing 1881 text Basil Stockmar, the book agent and
Hamlet's foster brother, exists beside the action of Shake-
speare's play. The only character he encounters directly is the
ghost of Hamlet's father, and the ghost does not speak to him.
With old satchel, old umbrella, and "weary with tramping,"
Basil comes on stage for a long speech to precede act 1. He is

"the farmer's humble baby" who has not seen Hamlet for twenty-three years, but if he "could see him biting at a rattle," he "would recognize him in a minute." His hope is that Hamlet and his mother will head the list of subscribers on the book for which he is canvassing and thus insure his success. "Just you let me get old mammy Hamlet's little old signature scratched down on this-here list of mine. . . ."

Perhaps the most effective part of the opening soliloquy is Basil's rehearsal of his "canvassing lesson," which he can rattle off "like a furniture auction." A high-flown sales pitch, the speech is straight from the nineteenth-century book trade, but the character here speaks in an innocent vernacular.

> Sir, it is a work which the family circle cannot afford to be without. Let me call your worship's particular attention to this admirable chapter upon 'The Mythological Era of Denmark'—and to this one upon 'Denmark's High Place Among the Historical Empires of Antiquity'; and *most* particularly to this noble, and beautiful, and convincing dissertation upon the old, old vexed question, "Inasmuch as Methuselah lived to the very building of the Ark and the very day of the flood, how was it he got left"?

Basil's rehearsal of his speech on this book, which is "just tip-top" and "lays over anything you ever saw," will conclude, he hopes, with a successful sale, an event which will bring out the masses: "They'll swarm around and say, 'No, but *did* 'er majesty look at this very picture, with 'er very own eyes?—how nice! And *did* sweet prince Hamlet say, with his very own mouth, that if he had his choice between this book and a barrel of di'monds, he wouldn't hesitate a minute to say 'O rot the di'monds, gimme the book?' "

Twain condensed the opening scene where Bernardo, Horatio, and Marcellus see the ghost, but he did not alter Shakespeare's own lines. Basil is not seen by Shakespeare's characters but he does have three slapstick encounters with the ghost. In one of these he "follows the Ghost's form up to its face with his eyes and then sneaks trembling away." In another, he says, "I don't think much of a country where they let a dead policeman go swelling around that way, nights . . . I reckon I begin to see what he was chasing me around like that, for . . . he wanted to *subscribe*. I'll just set him down for a couple of copies, anyway. . . ."

In his working notes for the burlesque, Twain indicated that he would have Basil assume an active role in persuading Laertes to go to France, Polonius to give Laertes leave, and the king and queen not to let Hamlet go to Wittenberg. In the existing lines, however, Basil assumes that he has accomplished these goals, but he does not talk to Shakespeare's characters. He seems to have forgotten about his book subscriptions as well, for his aim now, in the opening speech of act 1, scene 2, is "to break up this love match of Hamlet's and Ophelia Polonius's." As the action of *Hamlet* progresses, Basil is brought in to speak aside remarks, commenting on the appearance of the ghost:

Ham. What, looked he frowningly?
Hor. A countenance more
  In sorrow than in anger.
Ham. Pale, or red?
Hor. Nay, very pale.
Basil (Aside). Ugh! it ain't no *name* for it!
Ham. And fixed his eyes upon you?
Hor. Most constantly.
Ham. I would I had been there.
Basil (Aside). There was *one* front seat he could'a got cheap.

Basil's opening speech for act 1, scene 3 burlesques Shakespeare's language:

They swell around, and talk the grandest kind of book-talk, and look just as if they were on exhibition. It's the most unnatural stuff! Why, it ain't *human* talk; nobody that ever lived, ever talked the way they do. Even the flunkies can't say the simplest thing the way a human being would say it. "Me lord hath given commandment, sirrah, that the vehicle wherein he doth of ancient custom, his daily recreation take, shall unto the portal of the palace be straight conveyed; the which commandment, mark ye well, admitteth not of wasteful dalliance, like to the tranquil mark of yon gilded moon atwart the dappled fields of space, but, even as the molten meteor cleaves the skies, or the red-tongued bolts of heaven, charged with death, to their dread office speed, let this, me lord's commandment, have instant consummation!" Now what d———d rot that is! Why, a man in his right mind would simply say, "Fetch the carriage, you duffer, and *hump* yourself!"

Basil's vernacular perspective here has more criticism in it than the voice of Huck Finn, who might reach the same conclusion after an innocent appreciation of the Duke's grand style. Basil's final appearance has little relationship to Shakespeare's text and returns to the low comedy of his encounters with the ghost. Twain had made a note in 1880 about a "tight man who had swallowed a small ball of thread and stood pulling it out, yard after yard and swearing to himself." Here Basil, "pretty tight . . . has the end of the thread in his fingers and talks along disjointedly while he pulls out a couple of hundred yards of it." Though he continued to remind himself of this project in his notebook, Twain gave up on his burlesque of *Hamlet,* probably sensing that it lacked coherence. As late as 1897, though, he suggested that "H and the others to be allowed to speak to him now and then in stately form . . . 25 years ago Edwin Booth told me to *do* this. I tried and couldn't succeed."[25]

Perhaps the greatest value of Twain's attempted *Hamlet* was the preparation it gave him for what is certainly his most successful use of Shakespeare—the Duke's burlesque, or *pastiche,* in chapter 21 of *Huckleberry Finn.* With his background as the "word-renowned Shakespearean tragedian, Garrick the Younger, of Drury Lane, London," the Duke has already "learned" the Dauphin the sword-fight from *Richard III* and the balcony scene in *Romeo and Juliet.* For the Dauphin's proposed encore, they settle on "Hamlet's soliloquy . . . the most celebrated thing in Shakespeare." Since the Duke doesn't have the text for Hamlet, he calls it back "from recollection's vaults." Huck describes his effort: ". . . he strikes a most noble attitude, with one leg shoved forwards, and his arms stretched away up, and his head tilted back, looking up at the sky; and then he begins to rip and rave and grit his teeth; and after that, all through his speech, he howled, and spread around, and swelled up his chest, and just knocked the spots out of any acting ever *I* see before."[26]

The garbled nature of the Duke's soliloquy can be noted by

general line references to *Hamlet, Macbeth,* and *Richard III,*
though Twain on several occasions changed a word or phrase.
Huck says, "I learned it, easy enough, while he was learning it to
the king":

> To be, or not to be; that is the bare bodkin (*Hamlet* 3.1.56, 76)
> That makes calamity of so long life; (H 3.1.69)
> For who would fardels bear, till Birnam wood do come to Dun-
>   sinane, (H 3.1.76; *Macbeth* 5.5.45–46)
> But that the fear of something after death (H 3.1.78)
> Murders the innocent sleep, (M 3.2.36)
> Great nature's second course, (M 2.2.39)
> And makes us rather sling the arrows of outrageous fortune
>   (H 3.1.58)
> Than fly to others that we know not of. (H 3.1.82)
> There's the respect must give us pause: (H 3.1.68)
> Wake Duncan with thy knocking! I would thou couldst; (M 2.2.74)
> For who would bear the whips and scorns of time, (H 3.1.70)
> The oppressor's wrong, the proud man's contumely, (H 3.1.71)
> The law's delay, and the quietus which his pangs might take,
>   (H 3.1.72, 75, 79)
> In the dead waste and middle of the night, when churchyards yawn
>   (H 1.2.198; 3.2.407)
> In customary suits of solemn black, (H 1.2.78)
> But that the undiscovered country from whose bourne no traveler
>   returns, (H 3.1.79–80)
> Breathes forth contagion on the world, (H 3.2.407–08)
> And thus the native hue of resolution, like the poor cat i' the adage,
>   (H 3.1.84; M 1, 7, 45)
> Is sicklied o'er with care, (H 3.1.85)
> And all the clouds that lowered o'er our housetops, (*Richard III* 1,
>   1, 3)
> With this regard their currents turn awry, (H 3.1.87)
> And lose the name of action. (H 3.1.88)
> "Tis a consummation devoutly to be wished. But soft you, the fair
>   Ophelia: (H 3.1.63–64, 88–89)
> Ope not thy ponderous and marble jaws, (H 1.4.50)
> But get thee to a nunnery—go! (H 3.1.142–43)

These are famous lines, but Twain's ability to leap about with
this facility in Shakespeare is impressive, especially if he, like

the Duke, was working from "recollection's vaults." Walter
Blair reprints the nearly complete draft of the speech which he
believes Twain wrote in New York (March 19, 1883) on the un-
used portion of an opera invitation to "Aunt Livy" from their
nephew Charles Webster. According to Blair, this draft, written
"from memory it appears" was inserted into chapter 21 with only
a few minor changes.[27] In a brief but close reading of the text
itself Bruce Kirkham has since argued that the speech should be
read as an original, coherent composition, "not as a hodgepodge
of lines Twain tossed together from memory, but one he carefully
worked out with a text by his side."[28] Some of his reasoning is
perhaps questionable; for example, he suggests that Twain's
substitution of "waste" for "vast" is the sort of error one might
make if he were reading and copying from a text; this may be
true, but Twain makes exactly the same "error" in the *Hamlet*
burlesque. Yet his general conclusion—that the speech has
significance in the novel beyond its humor—is clearly supported
by Blair and others. Baetzhold asserts that

> whatever its immediate inspiration, the Duke's garbled soliloquy,
> with its wild *non sequiturs* that just miss being meaningful, is a more
> unified piece of burlesque than those already mentioned. More im-
> portant . . . this farcical treatment of Hamlet's musings on the nature
> of death is significant dramatically and thematically in *Huckleberry
> Finn*. Not only does it add another fact to the Duke's fraudulent
> character, but it also introduces succeeding episodes . . . which end
> in violence and murder.[29]

The originality and coherence of the speech give it a dimension that its models in Southwest humor do not match. Bernard
DeVoto points out that "mutilations of Shakespeare can be met
with everywhere in this literature," citing especially *The Theatrical Journey-Work and . . . Recollections of Sol Smith* (1854).
According to DeVoto, Twain was "well-acquainted" with
Smith's work, much of which had appeared in *The Spirit of the
Times*.[30] In one instance, Smith records a member of his company reciting the "seven ages of man" from *As You Like It* while
he is bumped and jostled by a waiter coming and going through a
kitchen door. The speech juxtaposes lines from Shakespeare

with comments to the writer and audience. This, however, is closer to Ealer's "What man dare, I dare," cited earlier, than to the Duke's soliloquy. Twain did use material from Southwest humorists in this section of *Huckleberry Finn,* especially for the Duke's comic posters advertising the Shakespearean perform-ance:

Shaksperean Revival!!!
Wonderful Attraction!
For One Night Only!
The world renowned tragedians
David Garrick the younger, of Drury Lane Theatre, London
and
Edmund Kean the elder, of the Royal Haymarket Theatre,
White Chapel, Pudding Lane, Piccadilly, London, and the
Royal Continental Theatres, in their sublime
Shaksperean Spectacle entitled
The Balcony Scene
in
Romeo and Juliet!!!

. . . .

Also:
(by special request)
Hamlet's Immortal Soliloquy!!
By the Illustrious Kean!
Done by him 300 consecutive nights in Paris!
For One Night Only,
On account of imperative European engagements!

Blair and DeVoto point out the special influence of Joseph M. Field's *The Drama in Pokerville* (1847) on the playbill, for his "Great Small Affair Company," performing in a southern town like Bricksville, announces an actor from "the Drury Lane Theatre, London," and an actress appearing for "the last engage-ment which she will perform prior to her departure for Europe."[31] Twain's own advertisements for his early lectures in San Francisco adopted the same burlesque tone.

The Duke's soliloquy may, like the playbill, be rooted in Southwest humor, but its originality, its uniqueness, lies in its coherent relationship to the Duke's character and to the larger

events of the novel. Bruce Kirkham's excellent reading of the
speech emphasizes its call to action, with action/inaction being
broad themes in both the novel and the plays, and he sees a
fundamental irony in the fact that a man with the Duke's moral
character "should give the very moral advice that Huck most
needs."[32] The Duke's soliloquy is also about Death and the
meaninglessness of modern existence. Without risking a paraphrase of Twain's burlesque here, I might point out that life has
no meaning in the Duke's value system, and that this *memento
mori* speech is something of a lament for his predicament in the
universe and perhaps an *apologia* for his lack of moral scruples.
He might "devoutly" wish to have the courage "to be," but such
a possibility seems impossible in the "calamity" of a world
where death "breathes forth contagion." In such "dead waste,"
he has no sense of responsibility, but will "sling the arrows of
outrageous fortune," back in its face, presumably, or at anyone
else. In contrast, Huck is a moral character who cares about
others a great deal, as his famous decision about Jim demonstrates. Twain's ambivalence allows him to use Shakespeare
here much as Shakespeare used Holinshed and other sources.
He has now "made free with Shakespeare," but it is not any lack
of respect (though the burlesque is overt) for his model which
readers of *Huckleberry Finn* finally notice. Instead, the Duke's
evil character is measured against the eternal values of being and
nothingness in a speech which becomes an original creation, and
he is judged accordingly. Twain gives his character a wildly
funny speech that is memorable for such nonsensical images as
Ophelia's "ponderous and marble jaws," but it tells us much
about the Duke as well.

Twain's last statement on Shakespeare, and also his most direct, is the essay *Is Shakespeare Dead?* (1909), published the
year before his death.[33] His interest of "fifty years," he says, in
the Shakespeare–Bacon controversy was rekindled by his reading of George Greenwood's Baconian views in *The Shakespeare
Problem Restated* (1908). During the winter of 1908–09 he concentrated on the Shakespeare–Bacon problem, reading both
Greenwood's book and proofs of William Stone Booth's *Some
Characteristics of Francis Bacon*. He apparently worked out

some of the acrostic signatures himself, and he dictated the manuscript of *Is Shakespeare Dead?*, supposedly to be included in his autobiography. His decision to publish the essay as a separate monograph is good evidence of how intense his interest in Shakespeare and Bacon had become. As Hamlin Hill points out the essay was not well received, especially by Greenwood who thought he was not given proper credit for the twenty-two pages Twain quotes from his book. Hill notes that the *New York Times* (June 9 and 10, 1909) gave the essay a scathing review, focusing on the sensational news of literary theft.[34]

Some critics, including the reviewer in the *Independent* and Minnie Brashear, have believed that the essay is a parody, a "skit to hoist the Baconians with their own petard."[35] The tone of the essay, though humorous, does not really suggest that it is a "skit," and DeLancey Ferguson admits that "it might have been better if it had been."[36] Despite its heavy reliance on Greenwood's book, the essay has characteristic Twain touches— jocular wit, humorous exaggeration, informality, and a reliance on memory—but it seems straightforward, not ironic, in its argument. Paine says, indeed, that "Mark Twain had the fullest conviction as to the Bacon authorship of the Shakespeare plays."[37] It might be, of course, that Twain plays a game with both sides here, demonstrating the foolishness of the argument.

After a brief discussion of Shakespeare as "claimant," *Is Shakespeare Dead?* begins with Twain's memory of his introduction to the Baconian question by the pilot George Ealer. Ealer not only read Shakespeare to Twain by the hour but defended Shakespeare's authorship "with heat." Ealer "bought the literature of the dispute as fast as it appeared, and we discussed it all through thirteen hundred miles of river four times traversed—two round trips. . . . He did his arguing with . . . violence; and I did mine with the reserve and moderation of a subordinate who does not like to be flung out of a pilothouse that is perched forty feet above the water." However, for the sake of the argument with Ealer, Twain "let principle go, and went over to the other side," a position first taken "almost seriously," then "utterly seriously," then "lovingly, gratefully, devotedly," and finally, "fiercely, rabidly, uncompromisingly." Twain's favorite

Baconian argument, offered in *Is Shakespeare Dead?,* originated in his discussions with Ealer. This is the contention that Shakespeare "couldn't have written Shakespeare's works, for the reason that the man who wrote them was limitlessly familiar with the laws, and the law-courts, and law-proceedings, and lawyer-talk, and lawyer-ways—and if Shakespeare was possessed of . . . this vast wealth, *how* did he get it, and *where,* and *when?*" Twain turned Ealer's standard reply, "from books," on its head by demonstrating that only a steamboat pilot had a clear notion of pilot language.

Twain's essay has thirteen sections, including his reminiscences of George Ealer. He compares public "reverence" for Shakespeare, and the lack of inquiry about him, to the attitude of his Sunday-school teacher toward the characters of the Bible, even Satan. He sets down the limited "facts" of Shakespeare's biography, and contrasts them with "conjectures" and "assumptions." The facts are so few, and the conjectures so many, that Twain says Shakespeare "is a brontosaur: nine bones and six hundred barrels of plaster of Paris." Twain describes himself as neither a Shakespearean nor a Baconian, but a Brontosaurian: "the Brontosaurian doesn't really know which of them did it, but is quite composedly and contentedly sure that Shakespeare *didn't,* and strongly suspects that Bacon did."

Among Twain's personal concerns is the question of Shakespeare's "literary celebrity" among his Stratford contemporaries. Why was there not more notice taken of Shakespeare among his townspeople, especially at his death, since he, Twain, is well on the way to becoming an industry in Hannibal? "If Shakespeare had really been celebrated, like me, Stratford could have told things about him; and if my experience goes for anything, they'd have done it." Yet the "master-key" to the Shakespeare–Bacon puzzle, for Twain, is the question of Shakespeare's competence in the law, and he quotes liberally from Greenwood's book on this issue. Greenwood argues that the author of the plays "had a very extensive and accurate knowledge of law," and "was well-acquainted with the manners and customs of members of the Inns of Court and with legal life generally." As he revealed in his argument with Ealer, Twain holds that a writer must have firsthand experience to reproduce language accurately, and he contrasts his own "inside" knowledge of mining with that of Bret Harte, whose dialect is "artificial."

To the question, "Did Francis Bacon write Shakespeare's works," Twain says, "Nobody knows." However, he develops Bacon's credentials, citing his biography and manifold opinions about his abilities from Macaulay and Ben Jonson, among others. In the concluding sections of the essay, Twain admits that convincing anybody that Shakespeare did not write Shakespeare's works is impossible, given the nature of the "Reasoning Race." In the atmosphere which compels "everybody to revere their Shakespeare and hold him sacred," Shakespeare will not "have to vacate his pedestal this side of the year 2209." In a final postscript Twain again marvels at the lack of any biographical information about such a famous person, illustrating from his own experience with Hannibal friends that "a really celebrated person cannot be forgotten in his village in the short space of sixty years." Some of Twain's essay, especially that dealing with his own reputation, seems to be tongue-in-cheek, and he may laugh at the "reasoning" associated with such a debate. His point of view on Shakespeare, however, seems clear: Shakespeare is a "claimant" like Mary Baker Eddy or Tom Driscoll among others, real and fictional, whom Twain characterized as false.

There is a distinction, of course, between Twain's irreverence toward Shakespeare the claimant and his attitude toward the plays, which he continued to admire. Indeed, Alan Gribben's extensive documentation of Twain's uses of Shakespeare is exceedingly strong evidence of a lifelong attraction that went far beyond formal acquaintance. If George Ealer's idolatry was the stimulus, Twain's "university," so to speak, then his knowledge of the plays became intimate through careful reading (sometimes aloud), amateur productions, and a permanent love for the professional theater. The four texts surveyed here—"The Killing of Julius Caesar Localized" (1864), the burlesque *Hamlet* (1881), the Duke's speech in *Huckleberry Finn* (1885), and *Is Shakespeare Dead?* (1909)—reveal the breadth and depth of Twain's interest in Shakespeare. At the same time they offer a record of

his ambivalence toward the great tradition in literature and toward Shakespeare himself. Twain's vernacular voice, jux-
taposed against Shakespeare's Elizabethan language and high
tragedy, creates incongruity, the basis of his humor. His irreverent approach is defined in his apprentice writings such as "The
Killing of Julius Caesar Localized." Yet his attempts to complete
the *Hamlet* burlesque, and his failure in it, show that he did not
find it easy to "make free with Shakespeare," and that he was
not certain of his "scale of values." His most powerful use of
Shakespeare is the Duke's pastiche in *Huckleberry Finn,* where
he "makes free" in an outrageously funny speech that also measures the Duke's fraudulent character against eternal verities.
The Duke's speech burlesques Shakespeare, but it is an original
creation as well. By 1909 Twain had moved beyond burlesque.
He was irreverent enough to attack even Shakespeare directly—
the man if not the plays—though he is careful not to declare him
dead. He does, however, raise the question.

NOTES

1. Alan Gribben, *Mark Twain's Library: A Reconstruction* (Boston: G. K. Hall,
1980), 623–636.
2. For Howells' estimate, see *My Mark Twain* (Baton Rouge: Louisiana State Univ.
Press, 1967), 15–17. In addition to Gribben's excellent introduction (xxvii–xliii) on the
question of Twain's reading, see M. M. Brashear, *Mark Twain: Son of Missouri* (Chapel
Hill: Univ. of North Carolina Press, 1934), 196–234; Gladys Bellamy, *Mark Twain as a
Literary Artist* (Norman: Univ. of Oklahoma Press, 1950), 43 ff.; Walter Blair, *Mark
Twain and Huck Finn* (Berkeley: Univ. of California Press, 1960), 13 and *passim;* and
John Baetzhold, *Mark Twain and John Bull* (Bloomington: Indiana Univ. Press, 1970)..
3. Gribben, 623–636; Baetzhold, 255–62, 371–73.
4. See references in the three published volumes of *Mark Twain's Notebooks and
Journals,* ed. Frederick Anderson et. al. (Berkeley: Univ. of California Press, 1975), and
Twain's use of Shakespeare in the letters of Thomas Jefferson Snodgrass to the Keokuk
Post (1856–57) and the letters of Quintius Curtius Snodgrass to the New Orleans *Crescent* (1861).
5. Blair, 303, and E. Bruce Kirkham, "Huck and Hamlet: An Examination of Twain's
Use of Shakespeare," *MTJ* 14 (Summer 1969): 17–19.
6. "Is Shakespeare Dead?" in *The Complete Essays of Mark Twain,* ed. Charles
Neider (Garden City, N.Y.: Doubleday, 1963), 408. Additional citations are from this text.
7. Baetzhold, 255.
8. Baetzhold, 255. Twain saw Forrest in *Othello* as early as 1854 (Gribben, 630).
9. Sydney J. Krause, *Mark Twain as Critic* (Baltimore: Johns Hopkins Press, 1967),
30.
10. Krause, 28.
11. *Notebooks and Journals* 2:85–86; 3:13, 205–06.
12. Cited in Krause, 28.

13. Baetzhold, 256.

14. *1601, Conversation As it was by the Social Fireside in the Time of the Tudors,* ed. Franklin J. Meine (New York: Privately Printed for Lyle Stuart, 1938), 38.

15. *Notebooks and Journals* 1:561–565.

16. The definitive text is now in *Early Tales and Sketches,* vol. 2 (1864–1865), ed. E. M. Branch and Robert H. Hirst (Berkeley: Univ. of California Press, 1981), 108–115.

17. Baetzhold, 256.

18. *Early Tales and Sketches,* 108.

19. The definitive text is now in *Mark Twain's Satires and Burlesques,* ed. Franklin R. Rogers (Berkeley: Univ. of California Press, 1967), 49–87. Additional citations are from this text.

20. Blair, p. 301. For a fuller discussion, see *Satires and Burlesques,* 49 ff.

21. Cited in *Satires and Burlesques,* 49.

22. *Notebooks and Journals* 2:261.

23. *Satires and Burlesques,* 53. For a fuller discussion of Twain's relationship with Joseph T. Goodwin on *Hamlet,* see *Satires and Burlesques,* 51 ff.

24. *Satires and Burlesques,* 51n.

25. Cited in *Satires and Burlesques,* 53.

26. *The Adventures of Huckleberry Finn* (New York: Holt, Rinehart & Winston, 1948), 127. Further citations are from this text.

27. Blair, 302–03.

28. Kirkham, 18.

29. Baetzhold, 258.

30. Bernard DeVoto, *Mark Twain's America* (Boston: Houghton Mifflin, 1967), 254.

31. Blair, 303; DeVoto, 254.

32. Kirkham, 19.

33. Again, the text used for "Is Shakespeare Dead?" is in *The Complete Essays of Mark Twain,* ed. Charles Neider (Garden City, N.Y.: Doubleday, 1963), 407–454. Additional citations are from this text.

34. Hamlin Hill, *Mark Twain: God's Fool* (New York: Harper and Row, 1973), 216–217. See also John D. Gordan, "New in the Berg Collection," *Bulletin of the New York Public Library* 43 (1959): 205–15, for a description of Greenwood's book with heavy annotations by Mark Twain.

35. Brashear, 218n.

36. DeLancey Ferguson, *Mark Twain, Man and Legend* (New York: Charter Books, 1943), 316.

37. Albert Bigelow Paine, *Mark Twain, A Biography* (New York: Harper and Brothers, 1912), 1486.

Resounding Fury:
Faulkner's Shakespeare, Shakespeare's Faulkner

Timothy Kevin Conley

"A play like *Hamlet*"

At a New Orleans gathering of artists in the winter of 1921, a young and unproven writer seemed to hurl direct defiance at Shakespeare:

> Finally the conversation turned to Shakespeare and to *Hamlet*. It was only then that the little man in the corner spoke.
> "I could write a play like *Hamlet* if I wanted to," he said, and then lapsed back into silence.[1]

In 1921, twenty-four-year-old William Faulkner had served briefly in the Royal Canadian Air Force (RCAF), been a part-time student at Ole Miss and an even more casual postmaster, and had written an unpublished one-act play and several poems for the college paper. Nevertheless, he was ready to duel with Shakespeare. According to Faulkner, he was challenging a fellow thief. In an essay on Eugene O'Neill written in 1922, Faulkner asserts that: "It can be seen how Shakespeare ruthlessly took what he needed from his predecessors and contemporaries, leaving behind him a drama which the hand does not hold blood that can cap."[2] Some three years later in a letter from Paris to his aunt, he applied the same words to an unnamed story of his own: "I have just written the most beautiful short story in the world . . . the hand doesn't hold blood to improve on it."[3] He may have been just stealing a favorite phrase from his own essay; he might as well have been suggesting, consciously or not, a comparison with Shakespeare.

During his most productive years—from the composition of *Soldiers' Pay* in 1925 through the publication of *Go Down, Moses* in 1942—Faulkner engaged in his fiction in a dialogue with Shakespeare and the past. From the late 1940s on this ex-

change became public. Faulkner told a class at Ole Miss in 1947 that Shakespeare's work "is a casebook on mankind; if a man has a great deal of talent he can use Shakespeare as a yardstick."[4] In 1957 at the University of Virginia Faulkner explained how all writers hope to measure up: "A writer don't want to be as good as his coevals, or even as good as Shakespeare; he wants to be better than Shakespeare."[5] Just months before his death in 1962 he told Simon Claxton that "we yearn to be as good as Shakespeare."[6] Perhaps by the time he had finished *The Reivers* Faulkner was less interested in competition than in his own accomplishment. Nevertheless, like many southern writers before him, Faulkner believed that Shakespeare was his yardstick, his casebook, and his competition.

This tradition of looking to the past for literary models, sources, and rivals is of course not confined to the South. We do find, however, that what W. Jackson Bate calls the "burden of the past" is particularly heavy in the South. C. Vann Woodward calls this the "burden of Southern history." In part this is due in literature to the tradition of stage performances of Shakespeare. Samuel Clemens, for example, attended river town performances of *Richard III,* amateur productions of *Merchant of Venice* and professional productions of *Julius Caesar* in St. Louis, and performances of *Othello* in Washington, D.C. Likewise Shakespeare found a place in family libraries throughout the South: Sidney Lanier and Henry Timrod, for example, grew up reading and listening to favorite Shakespearean plays. Although Faulkner's interest in Shakespeare did not extend to academic or scholarly work (as it did with Lanier, William Gilmore Simms, and later John Crowe Ransom), it did extend to a thorough familiarity with Shakespearean verse—as did the interest of Clemens, Simms, and Lanier. Faulkner wrestled with Shakespeare, trying to elude his grasp while never losing contact with his verse. Simms wrote *Confession; or, the Blind Heart* as a conscious attempt to rival *Othello.* In one sense, we can view Faulkner's early work as an attempt to write "a play like *Hamlet,*" while Faulkner's characters attempt to define, conquer, and escape the past which Shakespeare's work so often represents.

Faulkner's Shakespeare

The young Faulkner received most of his immediate encouragement and guidance from his mother, Maud Butler. Her autographed copy of *The Complete Dramatic Works of William Shakespeare,* included among the several texts of Shakespeare in Faulkner's library, attests to his regard for both Shakespeare and his mother's instruction and to Maud Butler's concern for her children's education. Perhaps the one consistent advocate of her son's writing career, she created a literary environment for her family and encouraged all her sons to read, among others, Shakespeare. Faulkner's acquaintance with Shakespeare probably began in his early years and his biographer, Joseph Blotner, says that by 1907, when he was ten years old, he was an avid reader: "He might not be ready for the Plato and Aristotle she [Maud Butler] herself read from time to time, but there were Conrad and Shakespeare and Balzac. These might be difficult for him, but better that they should be too demanding than not demanding enough."[7]

Faulkner's interest may well have been stirred by a "monologue recital" of *Hamlet* offered by "Thomas C. Trueblood, A. M., Prof. of Elocution and Oratory, University of Michigan." This 1906 performance, which Faulkner probably attended, was only the beginning of his dramatic interests. In 1913 Estelle Oldham, Faulkner's future wife, and other friends formed the MAN Club—whose name, as Joseph Blotner notes, derived from the title of *Much Ado About Nothing.*[8] This ice cream social and dance group may well have recalled to Faulkner his earlier reading. Blotner says, "Tenth-grade William Faulkner kept on reading. Some of the books were mentioned in school, but more often they were ones Miss Maud had suggested or others that took his interest in Grandfather's library: volumes of Shakespeare, Fielding, and Conrad."[9] Murry Faulkner, two years younger than his brother William, recalls a similar interest in the stacks of that library:

> Later, as we advanced in school—and at the always-encouraging hands of Mother—we began a lasting acquaintance with works of Kipling, Poe, Conrad, Shakespeare, Balzac, Hugo, Voltaire, Field-

ing, and many others, each of whom brought enlightenment and pleasure to three boys in a small Mississippi town more than half-century ago.[10]

This enlightenment and pleasure took a more serious turn under the tutelage of Phil Stone, an Oxford lawyer four years older than William Faulkner. Stone's guidance may not have been consistently perceptive or progressive, but the importance of Faulkner's reading with Stone, especially from 1914 to 1920, can hardly be underestimated. Here again Faulkner turned to an unstructured course for his education; his aversion to academic strictures was lifelong, though his envy of the trappings was not. Robert Coughlan points out that Faulkner's fondness for extracurricular study contributed much to his knowledge of Shakespeare:

> To his elementary and eclectic education Stone added at least the outlines of liberal education, both orally (Stone has an oral gift, and a memory that enables him to recite whole pages verbatim [a gift which Faulkner approximated]) and through reading courses. First came poetry: Shakespeare, Swinburne, Keats, Shelley, and the modern Imagists; then the standard classics, such as Balzac, Thackeray, Fielding, Defoe, Dickens, and Conrad.[11]

Although Stone did introduce Faulkner to such writers as Swinburne, the Imagists, and later Joyce, he only reinforced Faulkner's fondness for writers such as Conrad, Balzac, and Shakespeare. Faulkner's younger brother John recalls both their mother's and Stone's influence: "What Phil picked for Bill to read was pretty much what she [Maud] would have chosen. Bill read Plato, Socrates, the Greek poets, all the good Romans, and Shakespeare."[12]

When Stone travelled to Yale, Faulkner followed, and in 1918 the two briefly shared a room. Blotner describes their nightly recitation sessions at which a "favorite was Shakespeare's eighth sonnet" ["Music to hear, why hear'st thou music sadly?"].[13] Although Stone's influence would later decline as Faulkner moved beyond his scope, this early training provided Faulkner with a more discriminating sense of Shakespeare's verse and a more thorough knowledge of the canon.

As several critics and biographers have noted, Faulkner continued his reading of Shakespeare through his brief experience as a RCAF cadet and his somewhat more extended career as Oxford's postmaster. These years (1918–1925) found Faulkner still reading under Stone's supervision and in fact publishing his first book of verse largely through Stone's aid. His continued interest in Shakespeare also moved him to register for an elective course in the major plays at the University of Mississippi upon his return to Oxford from Canada in 1919. Dr. D. H. Bishop was chairman of the English department and apparently a bit of a pedant, but neither his position nor his manner intimidated Faulkner, who, as Blotner puts it, was "something of a trial to some members of the faculty":

> During a session devoted to Othello, Dr. Bishop read a passage aloud. Then he looked at Faulkner.
> "Mr. Faulkner, what did Shakespeare have in mind when he put those words in the mouth of Othello?"
> "How should I know?" Faulkner replied. "That was nearly four hundred years ago, and I was not there."[14]

Although it was in large part a response dictated by Faulkner's position as resident cynic and decadent poet (he was at twenty-two a world-weary veteran of cadet training in foreign, albeit North American, parts), the remark bears the tone of Faulkner's later responses to many interviewers who posed similar questions about his own work. Though he seldom participated in discussions (he spoke "to no one unless directly addressed," says a classmate),[15] his interest in Shakespeare again extended beyond the classroom. Hubert Lipscomb, a classmate and long-time Oxford resident, recalls that "Faulkner had his own ideas in the interpretation of Shakespeare and frequently engaged in lively arguments with Dr. Bishop."[16] These arguments indicated both Faulkner's resistance to academic formality and his quite thorough familiarity with Shakespeare. Unfortunately, Dr. Bishop thought otherwise—course grade: D.

In 1947 Faulkner returned to the university in a more auspicious position. After considerable maneuvering by the English Department and Professor A. Wigfall Green in particular, Faulkner agreed to meet with selected literature classes at the University in American literature, creative writing, modern literature, and, interestingly enough, Shakespeare. No transcript of those sessions exists, but the notes of Richard Allen provide a reliable synopsis:

> A student, picking up earlier mention of Shakespeare, asked Mr. Faulkner to name his favorite plays by Shakespeare. *Hamlet,* he thought, is probably technically the best play, but his favorites were the Henry plays and *A Midsummer Night's Dream.* His favorite characters were Prince Hal and Falstaff. Shakespeare, it seemed to Faulkner, probably would have liked to be a prince and take part in tragic love, but, since he never got to, he wrote about it. Shakespeare also wanted to make money.[17]

As was often the case with Faulkner's remarks about Shakespeare, he appears to have been talking indirectly about his own life as well—perhaps substituting for or adding to "tragic love" the Civil War and World War I. This is too easy a reading, but more and more Faulkner measured his achievement by Shakespeare's, in addition to using his work as a "casebook." All the characters and plays that he named in this discussion appear in his fiction, and the response itself echoes in *A Fable.*[18]

Faulkner's public comments during these years re-emphasize his familiarity with Shakespeare. In 1940 Faulkner granted an interview to Dan Brennan, and what emerged was one of the more sympathetic and illuminating exchanges of his early public comments. To Brennan's inquiry as to "what books might a young writer read with profit," Faulkner responded: "Well, . . . there are Shakespeare's sonnets and *Henry the Fifth*—some Dickens, and Conrad's *Lord Jim* and *Nostromo.*"[19] In a 1941 letter to Warren Beck, one of the earliest academic critics to recognize his merits, Faulkner acknowledged his conversion from the aesthetic decadence of the late Victorians to the standards of the classics, as he moved from verse to fiction: "I had discovered then that I had rather read Shakespeare, bad puns, bad history, taste and all, than Pater, and that I had a damn sight rather fail at writing Shakespeare than to write all of Pater over again."[20] In a 1948 interview for the New York *Herald-Tribune,*

Joan Hutchens summarizes Faulkner's response to an inquiry about his current reading: "Not much reading, either except of 'the old books,' to which he goes back regularly: *Don Quixote, Moby Dick, The Nigger of the Narcissus* and Dickens; and he carries a one-volume Shakespeare wherever he goes, though he doesn't travel much."[21] Faulkner was soon to travel quite a deal, but the answer remained substantially the same. It became a regular part of the Faulkner repertoire by which he defended himself against what he considered unnecessary snooping. Whether he did carry the now famous one-volume Shakespeare, and this seems to be the first mention of it, is doubtful; that he did other reading is likely. Yet the reference to this core of old favorites seems to have been an accurate report.

In 1956 Faulkner again suggested his regard for the past to Jean Stein:

> If I had not existed, someone else would have written me, Hemingway, Dostoevsky, all of us. Proof of that is that there are about three candidates for the authorship of Shakespeare's plays. But what is important is *Hamlet* and *Midsummer Night's Dream,* not who wrote them, but that somebody did. The artist is of no importance. Only what he creates is important since there is nothing new to be said.[22]

Faulkner here affirmed his desire for the anonymity of art and for his own privacy while placing himself in a narrative tradition of which Shakespeare is the foremost member.

This scrupulous care for the sanctuary of an artist's personal domain, however, did not prevent Faulkner from giving counsel to the novice. His advice was consistent: "Never stop reading the Bible and Shakespeare," he advised Joan Williams, and similar instruction occurred at Nagano, Charlottesville, and West Point.[23] Persistent as well as was his fondness for reciting, a trait nurtured by his early sessions with Phil Stone: "Later on they began talking Shakespeare. When some of the guests tried to recall an obscure sonnet, he identified it, then went on to qoute what seemed to Joan Williams 'reams of obscure Shakespeare sonnets from memory.' "[24] At times it seems that no Shakespearean lines were obscure to Faulkner, and quite possibly few were. Faulkner began learning those lines in his youth from his mother, and he developed an intimate acquaintance with Shakespeare through the help of Phil Stone and his own reading. Faulkner's personal Shakespeare library at the time of his death in 1962 testifies to his regard: five complete sets of Shakespeare, two of which bear his autograph (a particular token of his esteem), as well as copies of *The Histories and Poems, Songs from Shakespeare, Tales from Shakespeare, A Midsummer Night's Dream,* and *The Tempest.*[25] Forty-one years before his death, Faulkner shook his fist at Shakespeare; in 1962, he seemed ready to shake hands with the Bard.

Shakespeare and the Early Faulkner

Shakespeare's influence is clearly though inconsistently evident in Faulkner's early poetry and prose. In 1922, three years after his troubled Shakespeare course at Ole Miss, Faulkner cited Shakespeare as proof of a literary theory:

> Some one has said—a Frenchman, probably; they have said everything—that art is preeminently provincial: i.e., it comes directly from a certain age and a certain locality. This is a very profound statement; for Lear and Hamlet and All's Well could never have been written anywhere save in England during Elizabeth's reign (this is proved by the Hamlets that have come out of Denmark and Sweden, and the All's Well of French comedy). (*EPP,* 86)[26]

From this remark, we might infer that these three plays were among Faulkner's favorites. Although they may have been, little in the poetry of these years suggests their influence. However, Faulkner was reading Shakespeare during this period; he noted in "Verse Old and Nascent" (1925) that in the early 1920s "Shakespeare I read, and Spenser, and the Elizabethans and Shelley and Keats" (*EPP,* 117). In fact, he read quite a bit in these years, often at the urging of Stone, and mostly in Housman, Swinburne, and the Symbolists.

Critics have taken the clues supplied by Faulkner and discovered evidence of these poets, and Shakespeare, in the poems. Noel Polk unearths borrowings from Amy Lowell, Aubrey Beardsley, Verlaine, Mallarmé, Edna St. Vincent Millay, D. H. Lawrence, and A. E. Housman.[27] Such a catalogue of disparate sources suggests a problem which lessens the value of much of Faulkner's early work—the synthesis of his reading, however remarkable, is not complete. Although he strikes several artistic poses, Faulkner had not found his distinctive literary voice, and this makes source-hunting at once easier and less rewarding. The borrowings stand out in works not fully unified.

If in these early poems and sketches we can identify one definite link between Faulkner and Shakespeare, we must look to poem thirty-two of *A Green Bough:*

> look, cynthia,
> how abelard evaporates
> the brow of time, and paris
> tastes his bitter thumbs—
>
> the worm grows fat, eviscerate
> but not on love, o cynthia.

The address to the moon ("cynthia," or Diana) signals a landscape characteristic of many of Faulkner's poems. The men beneath that moon may indicate his reading as well. The story of the love of Heloise and Abelard, twelfth-century philosopher and theologian, may well have been known by Faulkner through historical documents, but it is also likely that he knew Pope's "Eloisa to Abelard" or possibly George Moore's *Héloise and Abélard* (1921).[28] The poem does not suggest either work, however, and the "brow of time" seems to be Faulkner's own image. Too, Faulkner might well have known the mythological figure Paris through a number of works, including those of Homer, Chaucer, or Shakespeare's *Troilus and Cressida* and *Romeo and Juliet*. The reference to tasting "his bitter thumbs" also may originate in a scene from *Romeo and Juliet* in which the servants of Capulet and Montague exchange insults:

Sampson: I will bite my thumb at/them, which is disgrace to them if they bear it.
Abram: Do you bite your thumb at us, sir?
Sampson: I do bite my thumb, sir.
Abram: Do you bite your thumb at us, sir?
Sampson (aside to Gregory): Is the law of our side if I/say ay?

Gregory (aside to Sampson): No.
Sampson: No, sir, I do not bite my thumb at you, sir,/but I bite my
  thumb, sir. (Rom. 1.01.42–51)

The phrase (and the act) were commonly understood in
Elizabethan England as a sign of scorn or derision, and the
phrase still carries similar significance. Thus Faulkner might
have acquired the idiom from any one (or several) of many
sources. He alters the phrase here and elsewhere (in the short
story "A Courtship," for instance) so that all the bitterness is
self-directed: the forlorn lover creates a situation in which he
can blame only himself for his misery.

These suggestions of previous literary works give way to direct borrowing in the final two lines. The source is Rosalind's
advice to Orlando in *As You Like It*. Rosalind tells Orlando that
no man has died in his "own/person, *videlicet,* in a love cause"
(*AYL* 4.01.996–97), and to prove her point she cites the cases of
Troilus and Hero—both died in ways unlike the manner con-
cocted by "the foolish chroniclers of that age" (*AYL* 4.01.105).
She concludes by insisting that "men have died/from time to
time, and worms have eaten them,/but not for love" (*AYL*
4.01.106–08). Rosalind here assumes a cynical voice to test Orlando's affection. This detached, somewhat weary stance
typifies many of the poems in *A Green Bough*, as does the rather
tentative use of Shakespeare. Yet as he turns to the novels of the
following years, Faulkner moves away from this posture and
develops a more flexible narrative voice and a more sophisticated understanding of his relationship to the past.

In his choice of particular words and phrases for his first
novel, *Soldiers' Pay,* Faulkner seems directly and explicitly indebted to Shakespeare. The "dying fall" from Duke Orsino's
opening speech in *Twelfth Night* ("That strain again, it had a
dying fall"; *TN* 1.01.04) occurs again in *Flags in the Dust* (pp. 43,
56, and 184), and, as we shall see, merges with a metaphor
borrowed from *Henry the Fourth, Part I*. In *Mosquitoes* Dawson Fairchild, a voluble novelist modeled in part on Sherwood
Anderson, employs another favorite phrase of Faulkner's which
was likewise found in the earlier poems and sketches: " 'Balzac,

chew thy bitter thumbs!'" (*Mos,* 345). In *Flags in the Dust* Horace Benbow, the Jefferson lawyer who reappears in *Sanctuary,* is described as an old actor confident of his ability "while the younger men chew their bitter thumbs in the wings" (*FD,* 212).

These borrowings, or echoes, may only suggest the appeal of isolated passages to Faulkner. A pattern of influence, however, seems to emerge if we consider the recurrence of various forms of words and images drawn from Macbeth's "tomorrow, and tomorrow, and tomorrow" speech.[29] Although word count has its limits (and practical critics would probably resist any effort to use such a method to suggest influence), an examination of the various forms of "fret"—"fretful," "fretted," "fret," and "fretfully"—suggests the development of the sound and fury passage as a significant theme in Faulkner's work. In *Soldiers' Pay* the characters surrounding the dying Donald Mahon strut and most painfully "fret": his railway companion Cadet Lowe (*SP,* 50); his father, the rector (*SP,* 89); his fiancée, Cecily Saunders (*SP,* 130); her father (*SP,* 112); her mother (*SP,* 97, 140); and her brother (*SP,* 95); Januarius Jones, an extremely literate and lecherous visitor (*SP,* 62, 65); Joe Gilligan (*SP,* 172, 250); Mrs. Powers, Joe's love and briefly Donald's wife (*SP,* 36, 39); Mrs. Burney, an inquisitive neighbor (*SP,* 180, 186, 258); young boys (*SP,* 149) and dancers from the town (*SP,* 202, 204); and the portraits of Donald's ancestors (*SP,* 136). The word "fret" and its variations are clearly not confined to one character or situation; indeed, the entire novel seems a brief stage for these nervous actors. In *Mosquitoes* these seem similarly "fretful": Gordon, a sculptor (*Mos,* 9); Taliaferro, a befuddled friend of the artist and frustrated lover similar to Jones in *Soldiers' Pay* (*Mos,* 12, 13); Mrs. Maurier, patron of the arts and organizer of the cruise (*Mos,* 61, 133, 259); Theodore Robyn, her nephew (*Mos,* 45); Dawson Fairchild (*Mos,* 49) and his neighbor (*Mos,* 308); Julius, the Semitic man and friend of Fairchild (*Mos,* 322); and Mark Frost, the icy and untested poet so fond of "ghostly epigrams" (*Mos,* 329). Even the inanimate world seems to resound to the actors' steps: engines fret (*Mos,* 215, 216, 263) and "a faint fretful sound" echoes across the swamps (*Mos,* 213). In *Flags in the*

Dust Faulkner seems largely to forego this image, but Simon, the longtime butler to the Sartoris family, both frets (*FD,* 10) and finally can "actually strut" (*FD,* 419).

Of course the mere repetition of one word from the soliloquy, though perhaps suggestive, is by no means conclusive evidence of influence. Yet Faulkner employs other words from that same passage. In *Soldiers' Pay* the characters time and again repeat Macbeth's "tomorrow, and tomorrow, and tomorrow." They "trod their shadows across the lawn" (*SP,* 65; see also 313) and finally console themselves with dusty memorials. In *Mosquitoes,* art can signify nothing, and man at times is only a walking shadow. Faulkner had employed similar imagery in his poems; these references in the early novels seem, consciously or not, to form a pattern more consistently and explicitly followed in the later fiction.

Probably Faulkner became more proficient in narrative structure as he became more certain of his commitment to and ability in writing fiction. He developed more imaginative and more complex characters, in part because he developed a historical background for them. Although he would often return to that repertory company first assembled for these three novels, in the later work he explores more thoroughly their family history, and they thereby become more interesting. The cast of *Mosquitoes* is particularly attractive. Genevieve Steinbrauer, Jenny, may be an early version of the irresistible Eula Varner, and her repudiation of Taliaferro is just as final as Eula's dismissal of schoolteacher Labove in *The Hamlet.* Similarly the flight of Pat and David West, the ship's steward, seems an early rendition of the story of Charlotte Rittenmeyer and Henry Wilbourne in *The Wild Palms.* The brief history of the rise of Mrs. Maurier's ancestors is Faulkner's first treatment of the rise of the outsider, a plot he will later employ with Thomas Sutpen in *Absalom, Absalom!* The characters become more complex as their stories are expanded and their pasts explored.

This pattern is important for a study of Shakespeare and Faulkner because it suggests the direction of Faulkner's development. His prose grew stronger as he looked back and discovered the significance of the past. The themes of the later fiction do not depart from those of the first three novels, but they acquire force and depth through Faulkner's more intense scrutiny of the past. In *Mosquitoes* we find discussions of virginity and suggestions similar to the thoughts which plague Quentin in *The Sound and the Fury*. But much of the accomplishment of *The Sound and the Fury* which distinguishes it from *Mosquitoes* is due to Faulkner's development of a historical and literary context for his themes. He does this in part by a continuing examination in each of these novels of the relationship of his own work to Shakespeare and the literary past.

Faulkner began his first novel, *Soldiers' Pay*, in the early months of 1925 in New Orleans. Although his most immediate tutor was Sherwood Anderson, he seems also to have drawn upon earlier reading done under the supervision of Phil Stone. Critics have noted the presence of Swinburne, Housman, and Beardsley in the novel, as well as the possible influences of James Branch Cabell, Joyce, and Fitzgerald.[30] Anderson, in fact, was apprehensive of the obvious effect of Fitzgerald's work: apparently he cautioned Faulkner to stop reading anyone else's work while he was writing.[31] This advice was appropriate, for *Soldiers' Pay* is awkwardly and self-consciously literary. The many allusions and borrowings often are either gratuitous reminders of the author's reading or rather blatant guides for the reader.

The same weakness plagues Faulkner's use of Shakespeare, particularly in the opening chapter in which the drunken Joe Gilligan, his companion, and Cadet Lowe travel home from war. The alcohol releases a rhetorical exuberance in Joe which seems to disappear after this first scene. He calls the black porter "Othello" (*SP*, 24, 107) and twice invokes the ghost of Yorick:

> "Alas poor Hank!" (*SP*, 18)
> "Alas, poor Jerks or something (I seen that in a play, see? Good line) come on, come; here's General Pershing come to have a drink with the poor soldiers." (*SP*, 9)

In mid-allusion Joe switches plays: he becomes as inebriated as *Macbeth's* devil-porter. This role fits Joe's taste; he later will announce the train's red-caps: "Here's the bell-hops come to carry you out where the parade starts" (*SP*, 21–22). Although the allusions have an immediate and appropriate effect, the later characterization of Joe as a sincere but rather befuddled guardian, apparently wholly ignorant of literature, seems at odds with this first meeting.

These allusions, however, do not conflict with the dominant tone of the book. Much as in the earlier sketches and poems, Faulkner here seems to accept the weariness of Macbeth's "to-morrow, and tomorrow" soliloquy. Life for these characters is, according to Jones, "a continual fret over futilities" (*SP*, 62). Jones and the rector "trod their shadows" (*SP*, 65), and, at the novel's conclusion, three young men pass Joe, "aping their own mute shadows in the dusty road" (*SP*, 313). The steps of these walking shadows may be only faint echoes of *Macbeth*, but their path originates in the soliloquy. That first chapter establishes at least some direction for the novel, however contradictory the characterization: we move from Joe's tipsy porter to the futile shadows of the conclusion.

The catalyst for all the subsequent action, which is of the most tentative nature at best, is the inert figure of Donald Mahon. The novel's formula is essentially a description of the reactions of the friends and family to the ravaged shell of their hopes. What this precipitates is a tale of people brought together for brief hours only to be scattered and broken at the novel's end. As Mahon lies dying, he suggests Shakespearean lines. "Day became afternoon became dusk and imminent evening," he thinks, as he "dreamed down the world darkly toward darkness. And suddenly he found that he was passing from the dark world in which he had lived for a time he could not remember again into a day that had long passed" (*SP*, 292). The vision of the battle which ruined him and now leads him to death becomes a vision of absent love similar to that expressed in Shakespeare's sonnet:

> But when I sleep, in dreams they look on thee,
> And darkly bright, are bright in dark directed.
> . . .
> All days are nights to see till I see thee,
> And night's bright days when dreams do show thee me.
>
> (Son. 43)

The lover's sigh of longing has become the soldier's scream of pain in an example of reverse imagery.

Januarius Jones may also echo "The Rape of Lucrece" in the image of his embrace of Emmy: "the falcon breaks his clasp and swoops away swift and proud and lonely" (*SP*, 227)—the same metaphor associated with Tarquin as he is about to rape Lucrece. Although Jones incorporates Falstaff's bulk and verbal skill as well as Tarquin's lust, his clownish appearance and inflated rhetoric are symptomatic more of minor infection than of comic effect. Jones resembles a sinister Falstaff and a vulturous Tarquin making the most of the dying Prince Hal and his mournful ladies. This malevolent clown—a "thicker shadow among shadows" (*SP*, 242), a "huge portentous shadow among less shadows" (*SP*, 243)—haunts the idiot's tale of walking shadows as a grim reminder of eager lust and debased romance.

Much like Gilligan, the drunken veteran so familiar with *Macbeth*, Jones chooses Shakespearean lines to dazzle his audience. Joseph Brogunier notes that "the sentence with which Januarius Jones dismissed Donald Mahon as an insignificant person, 'Let him be Donald, then' (*SP*, 77), sounds like an echo of Lear's 'Let it be so. Thy truth be thy dower.' "[32] Although Brogunier hears echoes which remain rather faint, Jones does resemble a somewhat less romantic hero, but one equally gifted with words. "You are a shallow fool" (*SP*, 229), he tells Emmy, possibly drawing on the words of Richard III regarding Anne: "relenting fool, and shallow changing woman" (R3 4.04.431). Jones's verbal skill is shared by many of Faulkner's men—Dawson Fairchild, Horace Benbow, Mr. Compson, Quentin, the reporter in *Pylon*, Darl Bundren, Gail Hightower, Ike McCaslin, Ratliff, and Gavin Stevens. Often this facility leads down a tortured path of insanity, isolation, and death. At times, however, it may result in a tentative ordering of the world.

Faulkner's art, like Shakespeare's, is in many ways predicated upon these inherent tensions of artistic expression, and both explore the possibilities of the creative mind at work—idiocy at one end, rational control at the other. For Shakespeare, it seems, the one possibility yielded tragedy, the other, comedy. In his early fiction Faulkner is more typically caught in the ironic middle ground of the later Shakespearean tragedies and romances—

a fantastic world which threatens chaos at every point and suggests only a tentative reconciliation.

Jones is perhaps the first example of the treatment of this
theme. His relation with Emmy provides what lightness the
novel has. Emmy provides an early clue to what, with the "tomorrow, and tomorrow" speech, is the most thematically
significant allusion in the novel. " 'Yonder they come' " (*SP*, 93),
she says, heralding the approach of Donald, Gilligan, and Mrs.
Powers. Perhaps this is an offhand remark by an excited lover (in
terms common to the rural South), but in choosing this phrase to
describe the soldier's return Faulkner has suggested a source
from which he will draw several lines. In *As You Like It*
(1.02.147) Celia speaks such words to Le Beau as the court
assembles for the wrestling match: "Yonder sure they are
coming." In *Soldiers' Pay* the court—including its learned
jester, Januarius Jones—similarly assembles to witness its
own wrestlings with the problems of postwar disillusion and
death.

As You Like It may also provide a basic metaphor for this
postwar world. When the various groups of hardened veterans
and carefree youths strut manfully across the floor of a local
dance, the appearance of "the lighted porch was like a stage"
(*SP*, 196–97), and Jaques's seven ages of man echo through the
night. Faulkner has distributed this one role to seven representa-
tives: we have no infant, but we do find "the whining schoolboy"
(Robert Saunders), the lover "with a woeful ballad" (Cadet
Lowe and George Farr), a soldier (Joe Gilligan), the justice "full
of wise saws and modern instances" (the rector), "the slipper'd
pantaloon" (Januarius Jones), and, most painfully, "second
childishness, and mere oblivion/Sans teeth, sans eyes, sans
taste, sans everything" (Donald Mahon). The speech thus
merges with Macbeth's idiot's tale to provide the epitaph for
these dying players.

The importance of *As You Like It*, which may provide the
source for the name of Cecily Saunders, seems assured by an
allusion made near the end of the novel—one which Faulkner
had earlier used in his poetry. As Gilligan and Donald's father
walk through the dusty Georgia night, the rector searches for
some consolation:

"You are suffering from disappointment. But this will pass away. The saddest thing about love, Joe, is that not only the love cannot last forever, but even the heartbreak is soon forgotten. How does it go? 'Men have died and worms have eaten them, but not for love.' " (*SP*, 318)

Rosalind's exact words are: "Men have died/from time to time, and worms have eaten them/but not for love" (*AYL* 4.01.106–08). The consolation is scant, and the same realization that drives Quentin to suicide only leads Joe and the rector "townward under the moon, feeling dust in their shoes" (*SP*, 319).

Joe and the rector finally are silenced by this realization. Shakespearean words provide an epitaph for dead love, not a literary context for reflection and reaction. Gilligan, after the rhetorical exuberance of the first chapter, seems caught in this painful position: he can find no words, no verbal context to express his emotion. He could have won Margaret Powers, "only I couldn't seem to think of what to say" (*SP*, 309). Similarly Cadet Lowe could not complete his love song to Mrs. Powers (*SP*, 50), and a frustrated veteran at the dance "sought vainly for words" (*SP*, 199). In many ways their inarticulate gropings signal Faulkner's first extended treatment of the dilemma of the artist dealing with his literary predecessors.

One of the problems with this novel, however, is that the most sympathetic characters—Joe and the veterans among them—cannot confront that past. Since he has read widely, Jones seems capable of reflection, yet he is at best a lecherous harlequin. The rector, perhaps the most pitiable character who also elicits our admiration, is bewildered by his son's condition. Margaret Powers and Donald may be the most intelligent and worthy figures, but the former seems motivated by feminine mysteries of which Faulkner appears unsure, and the latter remains a force, not a character. Faulkner seems to have been frustrated by his own choices. Consequently, the allusions often seem gratuitous, and the effect of the past is only suggested.

Faulkner's first novel is surely not among his best; at times the dialogue is strained and the narrative slight. However, it does suggest possibilities for the use of Shakespeare as a "casebook" and for the exploration of a writer's relationship to the past. In part the comic plot of *As You Like It* is here reshaped into an

ironic tale of cosmic disillusion which isolates the characters
from the past. The woods of Arden become a small Georgia
thicket which cannot avoid the stings of the town:

> The thrush, disturbed, flashed a modest streak of brown deeper into
> the woods, and sang again. Mosquitoes spun about him, unresisted:
> he seems to get ease from their sharp irritation. Something else to
> think about. (*SP*, 309)

In Faulkner's second novel that sharp irritation and the problems of the artist are all we are given to think about.

Faulkner wrote *Mosquitoes* in the summer of 1926 as he was
vacationing on the Gulf coast. The characters, as Blotner has
demonstrated, are drawn almost wholly from his experiences
among the artists in New Orleans. Michael Millgate calls the
work "a kind of rag-bag into which he could gather up all the
usable odds-and-ends of his brief literary past."[33] The jumbled
uses of this literary past create a novel which resembles, as
several critics have noted, the work of Aldous Huxley; it is a
novel of artistic ideas based largely on the author's own experience. Faulkner here also suggests Eliot's "Prufrock" and, in
descriptive passages, Conrad and Joyce.[34] Much like *Soldiers'
Pay*, *Mosquitoes* also resounds with titles and authors from
Faulkner's own reading. But unlike *Soldiers' Pay*, *Mosquitoes*
offers few echoes or allusions to suggest Shakespeare's presence.

There are, nonetheless, some indications of Shakespearean
verse. Richard Adams finds a link to *Macbeth*: "the symbolism
of the 'uneven dust' [*Mos*, 204] is vague, but its relation to
Quentin's section of *The Sound and the Fury* is reinforced by
Fairchild's later suggestion of Macbeth's speech, 'that there are
shadowy people in the world, people to whom life is a kind of
antic shadow' " (*Mos*, 231).[35] Several other speeches suggest
these lines. As noted earlier the characters, like those of *Soldiers' Pay*, fretfully pass their hours on the boat and their days in
the studio. The result of this artistic effort, however, may only
echo the idiot's tale:

> "Yes," agreed Mrs. Maurier. "How beautiful. What—what does it
> signify, Mr. Gordon?"
> "Nothing, Aunt Pat," the niece snapped. (*Mos*, 26)

Faulkner also suggests the "brief candle" as Taliaferro attempts to find his way down the stairs of Gordon's apartment (*Mos*, 13 and 21) and, in the same section which Adams referred to, Macbeth's "walking shadows":

> Their [Pat and David's] merged shadow blended at intervals with the shadow of the tall topless trees, but beyond the shadow of the trees their blended shadow appeared again, two paces ahead of him. (*Mos*, 205)

If the deck of the ship resembles Macbeth's brief stage, Faulkner has fittingly provided what Brogunier calls "Shakespearean stage directions."[36] The "voices without, alarums and excursions" (*Mos*, 193) which move Faulkner's poor players indicate an Elizabethan play-within-the-book. In Fairchild's later caricature of Taliaferro's misadventures before a God "above the excursions and alarums" (*Mos*, 345), Faulkner encloses life within a minor stage—brief moments of fretful posture.

In at least one of these scenes in the novel Faulkner draws upon his own experience both in Oxford and in New Orleans. Fairchild's account of his misspent days at "a kind of funny college" in Indiana combines both Faulkner's use (not portrait) of Sherwood Anderson and his own brief stay at the University of Mississippi:

> They were a bunch of brokendown preachers: head full of dogma and intolerance and a belly full of big meaningless words. English literature course whittled Shakespeare down because he wrote about whores without pointing a moral, and one instructor always insisted that the head devil in *Paradise Lost* was an inspired prophetic portrait of Darwin, and they wouldn't touch Byron with a ten foot pole, and Swinburne was reduced to his mother and his old standby, the ocean. (*Mos*, 116)

Poor Dr. Bishop. Faulkner's experiences in the classroom had left him a bit skeptical of academia, particularly when it violated the sanctity of his favorite authors.

Fairchild again speaks for artistic integrity when he instructs Mrs. Wiseman and her brother:

> "But women have done some good things," Fairchild objected. "I've read—

"They bear geniuses. But do you think they care anything about the pictures and music their children produce? That they have any other emotion than a fierce tolerance of the vagaries of the child? Do you think Shakespeare's mother was any prouder of him than, say, Tom o' Bedlam's?" [Julius said.]

"Certainly she was," Mrs. Wiseman said. "Shakespeare made money."

"You made a bad choice for comparison," Fairchild said. "All artists are kind of insane." (*Mos,* 247–48)

He indicates here both the intensity of artistic conception—inspiration perhaps, but more likely possession—and the ends of rational analysis to which an artist is driven. Although Fairchild's sunny exuberance and Mark Frost's rather chilly pride do little to suggest the torment and doubts which such creation can entail, Faulkner is constantly probing the degree to which any artist can analyze experience and successfully express that analysis. Unfortunately, in *Mosquitoes* that probing at times takes the form of statement rather than dramatization.

The cruise itself seems to provide little evidence of serious action. The satiric treatment of the affected pose of Mrs. Maurier and her entourage mitigates whatever tragic depth is present in their plight. Her invocation of lunar melancholy " 'Ah, Moon, poor weary one' " (*Mos,* 96), may be a forlorn echo of Helena's lovelorn address in *A Midsummer Night's Dream:* "O weary night, O long and tedious night,/Abate thy hours! Shine, comforts, from the east,/That I may back to Athens by daylight" (*MND* 3.02.431–33). After her yacht is stranded on the sandbar for a few hours, Mrs. Maurier wants to get back to New Orleans by daybreak. The entire cruise seems a perverse midsummer night's idyll, threatened by the characters' own short tempers and those ever-present mosquitoes.

Faulkner is thus developing his particular brand of Shakespearean comedy. In *Soldiers' Pay* the allusions to *As You Like It* signalled the thematic direction of the novel, and here the same play has its relevance. The "green world" in Shakespeare, though impossible to sustain, provided a temporary refuge in which man and nature were reconciled and from which man could return to civilization to restore balance and order. In *Mos-*

quitoes that Arden wood is a Louisiana swamp which affords no protection for the would-be lovers and from which they retreat to the same fretful society in a return heralded only by sexless regret. Rosalind's lines again appear as commentary on the scene:

> "Drowned himself for love?" Mark Frost said. "Not in this day and time. People suicide because of money and disease: not for love." (*Mos,* 227)

Faulkner returned to this theme again and again in his novels. His conception of a sanctuary to which man can flee but never remain is a major theme in his work, and it may be his own version of Shakespearean comedy.

The bulk of *Mosquitoes,* however, seems more clearly indebted to Huxley and the social comedy of ideas than to Shakespeare. The cruise provides Faulkner with an opportunity to juggle various concepts of art and life. Although the performance does not uniformly entertain, the act was one way for him to balance his own achievement (and that of his contemporaries) with the works of the past.

In this novel we find a novelist (Dawson Fairchild) whose only current work is a tall tale of the Louisiana swamps, a ghostly poet (Mark Frost) specializing in future verse and insistent epigrams, a desperate spinster (Dorothy Jameson) whose one "syphilis book" of verse includes stanzas from *A Green Bough,* and their several acquaintances who respond to the discussion of art: Mrs. Eva Wiseman, her brother Julius, and those frustrated patrons, Mrs. Maurier and Ernest Taliaferro. Fairchild is certainly the most talkative, and at times his fumbling belief in the power of words, and his regret at the loss of that power, suggest Faulkner's later public statements and interviews. According to Julius, Fairchild lacks "a standard of literature that is international" (*Mos,* 242), a tradition which transcends the confident pose of nineteenth-century American authors. As Fairchild realizes at the conclusion of the novel, the true artist must be a "genius" able to experience " 'that Passion Week of the heart' " (*Mos,* 339). Only Gordon, the brooding sculptor who refuses to engage in the endless talk aboard the *Nausikaa,* creates in such spirit; only he actually finishes a work of art in the course of the novel.

Gordon succeeds in part because of an intuitive grasp of reality as artistic form, but also apparently because he is not confined by the "talk, talk, talk: the utter and heartbreaking stupidity of words" (*Mos,* 186). Again Faulkner has written himself into a corner: the words seem necessary to refine a conception of art, yet the words themselves paralyze the artists. In fact, the voyage leaves the troupe a bit frazzled but essentially unchanged. They return to the same New Orleans studios as fretful, as discursive, as they had left, and they remain engaged in the moment and unaware of the past.

In these two novels we find Faulkner depicting writers apparently oblivious to the past. He occasionally borrows a phrase or suggests a passage from Shakespeare and others, but he appears as unsure of his own position as his characters are. In his next novel, *Flags in the Dust,* he again tackles the problems of the potentially inhibiting power of words and the pain of artistic creation, but he also develops a tradition in which to place the dilemma and discovers a more vital use of Shakespeare and the literary past.

In the autumn of 1926, Faulkner apparently discovered that his "own little postage stamp of native soil was worth writing about" as he began work on a story of the Snopes tribe, which he entitled *Father Abraham.*[37] A few months later he put that work aside to begin *Flags in the Dust.* In the manuscript version he introduced a genealogy of the Sartoris family as far back as Aylmer Sartoris, who "followed Henry Plantaganet to Rouen and there met and married the Provencal lady who had borne him the first Bayard Sartoris, had slung [a Toledo blade] about the young hips of that first Bayard Sartoris who carried it to Agincourt . . ."[38] Although the genealogy was omitted from the final text, the allusion to Henry V, Shakespeare's play, and the historical context were not.

Quite early in the novel Jeb Stuart and the Civil War Bayard are described as "two flaming stars garlanded with Fame's burgeoning laurel and the myrtle and roses of Death, incalculable and sudden as meteors in General Pope's troubled military sky"

(*FD,* 15). *Henry the Fourth, Part I* opens with a similar description by King Henry of the recent wars and "Those opposed
eyes,/which like the meteors of a troubled heaven . . ." (1H4,
1.01.9–10). The verbal similarities and Faulkner's original
genealogy, which suggested his literary and historical concerns
at the time, indicate that this is a conscious attempt to link two
works, and the allusion is quite apt. The War of the Roses was a
civil war which left the same deep scars and undying resentment
as the American Civil War, and, in this novel, the first world war.
For Bayard the younger, that war in France had been another
confrontation of brother and brother, and he had somehow sur-
vived. In a time of peace, however, such soldiers are as much
out of place as the impetuous Hotspur.

The significance of this allusion seems strengthened by further
suggestions of that play, and, more important, by repeated use of
the imagery of falling meteors. Aunt Jenny describes young Bayard as "neither flesh nor fowl" (*FD,* 407), a phrase which echoes
Falstaff's words about Mistress Quickly, "neither fish nor flesh"
(1H4 3.03.127). Lucius Peabody, the aged and immense country
doctor, possesses in part the vitality and humor of Falstaff. And
Bayard, like Hotspur, is tormented by nightmares and the vision
of his brother (for Hotspur, the figure of Prince Hal—in ways his
fraternal counterpart or twin).

The recurring images of falling stars or flames, however, indicate even more vividly the influence of the play. The Civil War
Bayard's "brief career swept like a shooting star across the dark
plain of their [Jenny and his Christmas audience's] mutual re-
membering" (*FD,* 22). Young Bayard is driven to repeat somehow that career: he retells stories "not of combat, but rather of a
life peopled by young men like fallen angels, and of a meteoric
violence like that of fallen angels. . . ." (*FD,* 133). He resurrects
ghosts in a tale "like a glare of fallen meteors on the dark retina
of the world" (*FD,* 134).

Faulkner uses this passage from Shakespeare as a central image around which he clusters related images to describe Bayard's relationship to the past. Civil War Bayard and Jeb Stuart
are "two angels valiantly and glamorously fallen" (*FD,* 14), like
the aviators of young Bayard's tales. The angels fall brilliantly

from the heavens, and the meteors die in their own flames. So young Bayard is haunted by the vision of his brother's fiery crash (*FD,* 46, 280) and is driven to repeat that death and the death of his Civil War namesake. The nineteenth-century Bayard, like Jeb Stuart, "appeared as gallant flames smoking with the wild and selfconsuming splendor of his daring" (*FD,* 18). And that memory is kept alive by the tales of Aunt Jenny, Old Man Falls, and old Bayard: the past is reconstructed in literary fashion and assimilated in present action. So Faulkner again and again associates Bayard (and others) with falling matches or ashes (*FD,* 45, 48, 153, 192, 209, 250, 262, 276). Bayard burns his brother's relics (*FD,* 240), rides a flaming and flying horse (*FD,* 137–38), and seems mesmerized by the fading glare of Christmas rockets (*FD,* 396). Finally he dies in a fiery crash, while his wife protects his son from Aunt Jenny's attempts to "Sartorize" him: "to make of my child just another rocket to glare for a moment in the sky, and then die away" (*FD,* 410).

The image of the "opposed meteors" thus merges with another passage from Shakespeare: that "dying fall" from *Twelfth Night* of which Faulkner was so fond. John, Bayard's brother, was consumed in a dying fall (*FD,* 368–69), and the phrase itself recurs in a servant's song (*FD,* 43) and, in a slight variation, the flight of a thrush in "a dying parabola" (*FD,* 56). Horace Benbow—Bayard's brother-in-law and figuratively his brother, or twin, engaged in law—likewise envisions his spirit as a caged bird seeking flight and the inevitable "plummeting fall" (*FD,* 191) and hears his words sound "with a dying fall" (*FD,* 184). These passages foreshadow Bayard's doom (and in some ways Horace's) and, because the image is kept vivid in haunting tales of the past, suggest the theme of influence which becomes prominent in this work. Faulkner develops Shakespearean verse for both technical and thematic use.

He likewise adds another chapter to his critical discussion of Shakespeare in a conversation between Horace and his sister Narcissa:

> "Belle's a rotten correspondent," he added. "Like all women."
> She turned a page without looking up. "Did you write her often?"

"It's because they realize that letters are only good to bridge intervals between actions, like the interludes in Shakespeare's plays," he went on, oblivious. And "did you ever know a woman who reads Shakespeare without skipping the interludes? Shakespeare himself knew that, so he didn't put any women in the interludes. Let the men bombast to one another's echoes while the ladies were backstage washing the dinner dishes or putting the children to bed."

"I never knew a woman who read Shakespeare," Narcissa corrected. "He talks too much."

Horace rose and stood above her and patted her dark head.

"O profundity," he said. "You have reduced all wisdom to a phrase, and measured your sex by the stature of a star."

"Well, they don't," she repeated, raising her head.

"No? why don't they?" He struck another match to his pipe, watching her across his cupped hands as gravely and with poised eagerness, like a striking bird. "Your Arlens and Sabatinis talk a lot, and nobody ever had more to say and more trouble saying it than old Dreiser."

"But they have secrets," she explained. "Shakespeare doesn't have any secrets. He tells everything."

"I see. Shakespeare had no sense of discrimination and no instinct for reticence. In other words, he wasn't a gentleman," he suggested.

"Yes . . . That's what I mean."

"And so, to be a gentleman, you must have secrets."

"Oh, you make me tired." (*FD,* 185–86)

The reader may well agree with Narcissa, but for Faulkner the discussion contains many of his recurring ideas and a telling remark about the structure of the novel. Both in *Requiem for a Nun* and in later interviews, Faulkner notes Shakespeare's uncompromising realism; earlier in *Mosquitoes* he disparaged courses which "whittled Shakespeare down." This concern for fidelity to external reality is matched by a fascination with the language by which Shakespeare's protagonists attempt to probe the order of that world. Faulkner obviously enjoyed the dramatic tensions and the rhetorical eloquence of Shakespearean drama and would have the same complaint levelled against him which Narcissa fires at Shakespeare—"he talks too much."

Although this passage may be a narrative intrusion of undue

length, it does suggest another play and another theme. Horace earlier had described his blown glass as a "midsummer night's dream to a salamander" (*FD*, 180). The Pyramus and Thisbe interlude in that play may have a parallel in Horace's tennis match, after which he asks Bell's daughter for her evaluation: "Well, Titania?" (*FD*, 206). Neither Belle nor the fairy queen were impressed. In fact women in this novel are not very much impressed with either their men or the legends of their men. The men, like Shakespeare's characters, "bombast to one another's echoes"—and the echoes of the past—while the women go about their chores. Jenny sustains the Sartoris family; Mrs. Beard runs a local hotel—and her husband; Minnie Turpin, a country girl of resolute virginity, convincingly frustrates her suitor's impetuous advances. Women control the lives of their dreamy husbands, and they end the novel in charge of their husbands. If, like Aunt Jenny, they perpetuate the deeds of their men in romantic tales, they finally are not dominated by those legends. They go on; the men die. Literature is an escape for Jenny and at times for Narcissa, but it is not a burden.

The men, however, must bear the weight of the past, and Faulkner establishes that past as a literary burden. The novel's protagonists thus bear some resemblance to Hamlet. Lauren Stevens says that *"Sartoris is a romantic melodrama, a descendant of Shakespeare's Hamlet."*[39] The novel does have a Horatio left to tell the story, and in a sense Bayard Sartoris is a type of young Dane caught amid the ghosts and glories of the past. Hamlet contrasts the mean times of Claudius with the heroic reign of his father and sees only decline and ruin in Denmark. He himself cannot approximate the deeds of Hercules or rugged Pyrrhus; the heroic age is irrecoverable, and Hamlet's day offers scant possibility for true tragic dimensions. So too Bayard is haunted by the memory of Colonel Sartoris and his brother's death in the wars of better times. Bayard, like Hamlet, cannot bear the weight of "the doom he could not escape" (*FD*, 324). Horace too echoes Hamlet's lament for this "too sullied flesh": "living and seething corruption glossed over for a while by smoothly colored flesh" (*FD*, 337). Yocona County, like Denmark, is a garden grown rank.

Faulkner himself seems to have written the book in a spirit akin to Hamlet's. In an unpublished manuscript written in 1929, he says that in this novel he was trying "to recreate between the covers of a book the world as I was already preparing to lose and regret."[40] In this novel he attempts to recreate his immediate family history in artistic forms which repeat the phrases and scenes of his literary predecessors. Michael Millgate notes "this sense of the presence of the past and the power and palpability of the unseen";[41] tales and figures from the past and the inevitably diminishing present dominate the Sartorises. Peabody's son is an antiseptic shadow of his father; the McCallums, a country family to whom Bayard briefly flees, remain strong, yet lesser figures than their father, and their half-breed pets only mimic the gestures of General, the family's nobler hunting dog (*FD,* 375). For Faulkner too the task seems clear: how can he venerate and imitate his literary predecessors and at the same time create work of his own as estimable as theirs?

In part then the plot of *Flags in the Dust* is the plot of the artist tormented and driven by standards of the past—in this novel, often explicitly Shakespearean. Horace and Bayard, and Faulkner as narrator, painfully seek some accommodation with that past; they are artists in search of the complete and pure moment in which they may attain peace. The novel then may be seen as a study of influence as the protagonists move through war to surrender to their pasts.

Horace most obviously envisions himself as an artist. He creates glass vases and muses on his sister as a version of Keats's Grecian urn. Mythically he retraces Orpheus's steps as he descends into the underworld to reclaim his love—in this novel a descent into the caves in which he blows his delicate glass figures (*FD,* 180). Yet he cannot fully grasp the significance of his relationship with either Narcissa or Belle: he jumbles messages and fumbles for the "meaning of peace." Bayard likewise seeks artistic closure. His kiln is more threatening than Horace's, but he too must create that one act which will complete his war with the past. Horace suggests that Bayard, like his brother, may be a poet (*FD,* 201), but Bayard's role, unlike

Horace's, is initially upward. He is Icarus, finally plummeting from the sky in fiery death. Like Horace, however, he remains finally inarticulate when confronted with the past.

Horace and Bayard also apply to their lives the same terms by which Faulkner defines art, and so the author's grappling for a conclusion in view of the accomplishments of the past coincides with the protagonists' search for peace in the wake of their predecessors. In the Foreword to the *Faulkner Reader,* written in 1954, Faulkner says that when he turned to fiction he "discovered that my doom, fate, was to keep on writing books" (*Reader,* viii); in his 1956 interview with Jean Stein he states, in relation to his borrowings, that "an artist is a creature driven by demons." In the National Book Award address he speaks of the "dream splendid enough, unattainable enough yet forever valuable enough, since it was of perfection."[42] Horace and Bayard are both driven by demons, doomed to incomplete fulfillment of their dreams. The soldier, the lawyer, and the artist are alike frustrated. The quest seems defined by Faulkner in his interview with Ms. Stein: the artist "has a dream. It anguishes him so much that he must get rid of it. He has no peace until then."[43] In this novel Horace's search for "the meaning of peace" and Bayard's search for the peace which had already ended a war merge with the artist's anguish. The novel ends on "a windless lilac dream, foster-dam of quietude and peace" (*FD,* 433). Even that peace borrows its terms from another age and another poet; the spectre of the past haunts the very conclusion which should finally dispel it.

It has been necessary to move away from Shakespeare's immediate effect on these first three novels in order to establish Faulkner's growing awareness of the significance of the past—historical and literary. In *Soldiers' Pay* and *Mosquitoes* we find Faulkner occasionally borrowing phrases and images from Shakespeare, but we discover little evidence of the playwright's influence. In *Flags in the Dust* the image of the falling meteors, borrowed from *Henry the Fourth,* is so organically vital to the novel that we may begin to speak of influence. And in *Flags in the Dust,* Faulkner himself addresses that very problem of influence: how can his characters react to the present when the past dominates them, and how can an artist fulfill the expectation which the achievements of the past raise?

Faulkner grew increasingly concerned with what W. Jackson Bate calls the "burden of the past." In his best work, which with one or two exceptions he completed in the 1930s, he shows his characters struggling with that burden, and their relationship to the past provides much of the novels' strengths. In his later fiction (which includes the Snopes trilogy, the three Gavin Stevens detective works, *A Fable* and *Reivers*), he appears to have gained a secure place in relation to his literary ancestors, in particular Shakespeare. Faulkner never did write a play like *Hamlet*, but neither did he lapse back into silence.

Shakespeare and the Mature Faulkner

The Sound and the Fury, the first work of Faulkner's artistic maturity, is the fullest expression of Faulkner's considerable reading in Shakespearean tragedy, comedy, and romance. We find frequent allusions and suggestive parallels and echoes which point to Shakespeare's influence. We find as well the most complete expression of a theme borrowed from Macbeth's soliloquy that Faulkner developed and modified in most of his work.

This fact has not escaped Faulkner critics, as Richard Adams notes:

> The Shakespeare influence is almost equally substantial [to that of the Bible], and many critics have discussed it, particularly in connection with the "tomorrow, and tomorrow, and tomorrow" speech in *Macbeth,* from which the title of *The Sound and the Fury* comes and which is explicitly echoed not only in that book but in many other stories, including *Pylon, Absalom, Absalom!, The Wild Palms, The Hamlet, Go Down Moses,* the story entitled "Tomorrow" in *Knight's Gambit, Intruder in the Dust, Requiem for a Nun, A Fable,* and *The Town*. The "tomorrow and tomorrow" formula strongly expressed Faulkner's feeling for the endless burden of endurance that must be sustained if man, as the Nobel Speech predicts, will ultimately "prevail."[44]

Adams's identifications are correct, though not thorough, but his interpretation is limited, though not inaccurate. Faulkner alluded to this passage as early as 1925 in his New Orleans sketches and included references to it, (besides in those books cited by Adams) in *Soldiers' Pay, Mosquitoes, Flags in the Dust, As I Lay Dying, The Unvanquished, A Green Bough,* and many of his short stories: "Elly," "Wash," "Fox Hunt," "There Was a Queen," "Mountain," "Beyond," "Mountain Victory," and "Mistral."

The figure of the isolated, childless, and homeless Macbeth who faces imminent death with no hope of personal extension in time was a powerfully suggestive image for Faulkner. Perhaps the two characters who most vividly embody Faulkner's contrasting attitudes toward this figure are Isaac McCaslin and Gavin Stevens. At the end of *Go Down, Moses,* MacCaslin is a lonely old man beaten by time and his own heritage, and he echoes the despair of Macbeth. In *The Town* and *The Mansion,* Stevens is similarly isolated, but he attempts, with some success, to build that enduring home of love with Linda Snopes, and, more important, he bequeaths his vision of endurance to his nephew—an extension of self denied Macbeth and Uncle Ike. The two contrasting uses of the Macbeth soliloquy show Faulkner at his creative best. The idiots and poor players, victims of two wars and their own melancholy disillusionment, are more typical of the earlier, and in general better fiction.

Between 1929, the year *The Sound and the Fury* was published, and 1934, when he began *Absalom, Absalom!,* Faulkner completed four novels. Two of these, *Pylon* and *As I Lay Dying,* were hurriedly composed in less than six weeks each, and one, *Light in August,* was in Faulkner's words a "deliberately" composed novel. The fourth, *Sanctuary,* was "basely" conceived, in his terms, and written to make money. In *The Sound and the Fury* Faulkner could afford to ignore external pressures; but in these four novels the necessity to provide for his family and his awareness of his position as a professional writer forced him to acknowledge the demands of the market. He composed these works under financial and personal duress, and he created characters who themselves seem controlled by their situations: external conditions frustrate the literate spokesmen in these works. In *Pylon, As I Lay Dying, Light in August,* and *Sanctuary* we find particular characters capable of expression formed in part by Shakespeare's words. But we also find these same characters unable to develop their own strategies by which to structure their lives. The artist figure, the man with verbal sophistication and dexterity, is largely determined by external forces and is unable to offer direction or order.

In *Pylon,* the allusions to Macbeth's soliloquy seem too mechanical. Contemporary reviewers of the novel, if they did not immediately dismiss the novel as the second-rate performance of a third-rate talent, could not help but notice the chapter titles— "Tomorrow," "And Tomorrow," and "Lovesong of J. Alfred Prufrock"—suggesting the book's themes. Later critics have also noted these borrowings.[45] In *The Sound and the Fury* Macbeth's lines rise organically from the dramatic action; in *Pylon* Faulkner begins with these lines as a slogan and insists upon their relevance by continual reference to them. This method recurs in much of the later fiction, although the lines are adjusted to a different theme, and the effect is inhibiting rather than expansive.

Like *Pylon, As I Lay Dying* observes strict temporal limits; the action in both is confined to roughly one week. Both were likewise composed in roughly six weeks. *As I Lay Dying,* however, bears these limits much better than does *Pylon. As I Lay Dying* proceeds from a single, simple action, resonant of classical myth and occasionally Shakespearean verse. *Pylon* proceeds from Eliot's verse and a single statement, somewhat simply repeated, from Shakespeare's *Macbeth. Light in August,* although again a "deliberate" book, joins several actions and several chronologies and draws more fully upon various Shakespearean plays.

Faulkner developed a contrapuntal theme to that desperate sound and fury in the composition of the various sanctuaries to which his most harried protagonists flee. *Sanctuary* offers such frustrated refuge, and several other works contain this same theme in similar terms. In "Centaur in Brass" Faulkner suggests a temporary haven in which man can rest, though not reside: "there is a sanctuary beyond despair for any beast which has dared all, which even its mortal enemies respect" (*Collected Stories,* 165). In this story he allows natural man, the "beast," a refuge which he will more fully explore in *The Town: "a sanc-tuary, a rationality of perspective,* which animals, humans too, not merely reach but earn by passing through unbearable emo-tional states like furious rage or furious fear" (*Tow,* 27). In the early fiction such content was a birthright of idiots and beasts; in such later works as *The Town* and *The Mansion* it becomes both rational and earned: "the one sanctuary where at least once a week they could find refuge among the other betrayed and dis-possessed reaffirming to each other that one infinitesimal scrap had been so" (*Man,* 181).

In Faulkner's early novels man is too aged and ineffective for renewal in any sanctuary. In the later fiction his characters jour-ney to natural refuges, and the works end with the resolution of the individual crises and the restoration of order in society. This is essentially a reshaping of Shakespeare's comic plot of a jour-ney into the woods and a return to society. In this comic plot man moves from civilization and its restraints to the "green world" of license and release, and then back to society in order to reconstitute it according to a renewed sense of man's place in nature. The two most representative plays, says C. L. Barber, are *As You Like It* and *A Midsummer Night's Dream.*[46] Although these plays are among Faulkner's favorites, his vision of those woods and their place as man's natural sanctuary is considerably grimmer than Shakespeare's. Only in the later fiction does he move toward a union of comic plot and comic spirit. Yet even in his early work he employed three characteristics of Shake-spearean comedy: holiday setting, a journey from civilization to nature, and the scapegoat.

In Faulkner's comic pattern, misrule is a characteristic feature of society rather than a temporary refuge from it. As James Mellard suggests in "Caliban as Prospero," such idiots as Benjy Compson and Ike Snopes are limited to the natural part of man, and it is only such figures who are comfortable in Faulkner's green world.[47] Others, such as Henry Wilbourne and Charlotte Rittenmeyer from *The Wild Palms* and the crew of *Mosquitoes,* will attempt such retreat from civilization's restraints, but they are unsuccessful. In the early fiction, anti-comic society, whether constituted by the fiscally sound disorder of Jason Compson and Flem Snopes or the Keystone Kops ineptitude of the prison superintendent in "Old Man," remains untouched by the protagonists' flight.

Sanctuary signaled the beginning of Faulkner's most productive decade. Between 1930 and 1939, he wrote Hollywood screenplays, some forty short stories, and seven novels, at least two of which (*Light in August* and *Absalom, Absalom!*) are among his best. At times, however, external demands seemed to dictate the shape and scope of his work as much as did artistic rationale. As we have seen, he wrote *Pylon* and *As I Lay Dying* with a sense of financial and artistic urgency. Later in this decade similar pressure would surround many of the stories and two of the novels—*The Unvanquished* and *Go Down, Moses.* These external factors alone cannot account for a shift in either achievement or style, but after *Absalom* we do find a noticeable change in Faulkner's composition.

In terms of his use of and attitude toward Shakespeare, *Absalom* marks the completion of one phase of Faulkner's career. Quentin's final anguished reaction to the South: *"I don't hate it! I don't hate it!"* (*AA,* 378), captures Faulkner's own feelings toward his literary heritage. With the guidance and often frantic counsel of his elders, Quentin has constructed a tale of Greek and Elizabethan dimension which gives shape and meaning to his own creation.[48] So Faulkner draws substance from the past and weighs his own achievement by Shakespeare's. He appears also to release himself from the emotional burden of that achievement in Quentin's cry. The "tomorrow, and tomorrow, and tomorrow" soliloquy and Shakespeare's comic pattern of release and clarification remain significant elements of the later compositions. But after *Absalom* the allusions to and echoes of Shakespeare do not form an artistic burden; they provide literary formulas.

During the rest of this decade Faulkner's narrators, for the most part, look less often to the literary past for their models and rivals, as Faulkner himself turned during this period to social and personal concerns and to shorter forms. After *Absalom* he sought answers to the sociological problems of the South along with reconciliation of his own difficulties, and did not fully immerse himself in a novel until he began the Snopes trilogy at the end of the decade. Perhaps his necessary attention to the short story inhibited the genius of *Absalom.* Although this may not be sole cause, the effect on his writing is clear: each of the three novels of this period *(The Unvanquished; Go Down, Moses; The Wild Palms)* begins with a thesis and is organized into episodes. We have then two probable reasons for the shift in Faulkner's relation to Shakespeare and the past: psychological (the purging effect of *Absalom,* which seemed to establish his own voice in answer to the accomplishments of the past) and biographical (the financial necessity to devote time to short stories and collections).

In the midst of completing *Absalom,* Faulkner turned to several sources for immediate income. Several of these have been noted, *Pylon* and the Hollywood screenplays most notably, but his most persistent attempt to gain publication and funds was the writing of his many short stories. His early sketches in *The Double-Dealer* in the 1920s had attracted some attention; more important, they convinced him to pursue a career in fiction. By the mid-1930s his interests were directed primarily to the longer works, *Absalom, Absalom!* in particular, but he continued to seek (usually unsuccessfully) an outlet for his shorter pieces. These do not include allusions to Shakespeare as consistently as the novels do, but often the references are strategically located for significant rhetorical and thematic effect.

The Unvanquished originated in a financial crisis and was completed in Hollywood under duress. This does not wholly diminish the achievement of the work, but it does suggest a context different from that of *The Sound and the Fury* and *Absalom.* Faulkner suggested that the theme of the book was "Granny's struggle between her morality and her children's needs,"[49] and indeed the novel seems to have embodied Faulkner's own struggle between his personal code of morality and his family's and region's deeds. The novel proposes the moral dilemma of a family during and after war. Even more than *Flags in the Dust,* which supplied the subsequent history of the Sartoris clan, *The Unvanquished* draws upon the lives of the Faulkner ancestors, and it does so without the presence of a literary spokesman such as Horace Benbow.

In *Go Down, Moses* Faulkner depicts a wider range of characters, and he more frequently suggests Shakespearean lines, although finally Shakespeare is not a dominant influence. He includes pre-war landowners, slaves and their descendants, Indians and half-breeds, and the troubled McCaslin heir at various ages. Yet of these only Ike is sufficiently well-read to grapple with a literary heritage, and the book he reads is not Shakespeare but the commissary account book.

The novel moves toward social analysis more than literary reflection, as Faulkner's self-conscious narrators express social concern rather than literary anguish. The work at times is burdened by talk about the problems of the South: McCaslin Edmonds, Ike's fatherly cousin, and Ike himself seem bent on explicating the racial complexities in speeches as interminable as those aesthetic discussions in *Mosquitoes*. Faulkner's continual insistence upon man's ability to endure is here symptomatic of the tendency toward statement rather than dramatization which plagues his later novels and at the same time saved his Nobel Prize speech. When Ike cites Keats's "Urn" to explain to Edmonds his rejection of the McCaslin inheritance or when Faulkner echoes the "tomorrow, and tomorrow, and tomorrow" soliloquy in "Delta Autumn" to present Ike's final predicament, he is using his predecessors' lines as slogans rather than reacting to them as organic elements of his narrative. When he describes the trophies of the hunt "in the libraries of town houses or the offices of plantation houses or (and best of all) in the camps themselves" (*GDM*, 192), he offers a fitting emblem of his own relation to Shakespeare and the works of the past. *Flags in the Dust, The Sound and the Fury, Light in August, Absalom, Absalom!—*even *Soldiers' Pay* and *Mosquitoes*—were conceived in the library, and they bear living witness to the influence of those books. *The Unvanquished* is a plantation-house novel written in the Faulkner office and designed to sell. *Go Down, Moses* recalls the fires and tales of the hunting camps, those temporary refuges from personal, financial, and social troubles. Although in many ways these last two works are superior novels, in *The Unvanquished* and *Go Down, Moses* Shakespeare becomes a trophy of the hunt, no longer a rival, or friend.

Shakespeare may, however, have exerted friendly influence on *The Wild Palms*. This novel differs from both *The Unvanquished* and *Go Down, Moses* in its greater number of Shakespearean borrowings and echoes and in its genesis and method of composition. But still Faulkner was writing under considerable immediate pressure, although not primarily financial, and without Shakespeare's presiding influence. At home in the fall of 1937 he began the work, as he told Jean Stein, as "the story of Charlotte Rittenmeyer and Henry Wilbourne, who sacrificed everything for love, and then lost that."[50] In the course of their wanderings, Charlotte and Henry separate themselves from, and occasionally attack, Hollywood, children, romance, and literature. Their concern with literature is most pertinent to this study. Faulkner was especially disturbed by the pollution of his talents with what the character Henry calls "cheap money" (*WP*, 299). Henry writes sordid tales for the pulp magazines, and the effort tarnishes his love; dime novels betray the convict, and he ends in prison. For the most part those texts, not Shakespeare, dominate the novel. It seems as if in this novel Faulkner wished to purge himself of the effects of screenplays, magazine stories, and a painful love affair. In *Absalom* Faulkner sought some reconciliation with his literary heritage, and Shakespeare proved a vital influence. In *The Wild Palms, Go Down, Moses,* and *The Unvanquished* external factors dominate, and Shakespeare provides only slogans and distant parallels.

In the fiction of his last two decades (1940–62), Faulkner turned from the personal subjects of his earlier novels to a generally optimistic sense of human history. The eight novels of this final period may be classified into three categories: the Snopes histories, the Stevens mysteries, and the two explicit genre pieces, *A Fable* and *The Reivers: A Reminiscence.* With the exception of *The Reivers* (his final work) all these novels developed over a number of years according to a rather careful plan. More and more Faulkner seemed to move from a sense of the individual or family caught in a personal struggle with titanic forces, typical of the novels of the 1920s and early 1930s, to a sense of man as a part of larger historical forces—sociological, moral, and at times religious. In some ways the movement reverses Shakespeare's: the historic sense postdates the tragic for Faulkner.

In this later fiction Faulkner also adjusts his vision of man's potential and so refocuses his view of Shakespeare's comic plot. In *A Fable* the carnival atmosphere of "Spotted Horses" lightens the journey of the English groom and his stolen racer, but in this story natural force is controlled and exalted as the various country folk help the groom elude the law. The comic forces of unrestrained nature even modify anticomic society's statutes, and the English groom not only escapes but finally also returns to act toward a reconstruction of society. When the war-ravaged runner disrupts the memorial ceremonies at the novel's conclusion, he speaks for Faulkner's comic heroes who had so often been beaten by forces of established disorder:

> "Listen to me, too, Marshall! This is yours: take it!" and snatched, ripped from his filthy jacket the medal which was the talisman of his sanctuary and swung his arm up and back to throw it. (*Fab,* 380)

Although anti-comic society remains in power, the man who has achieved some reordering of his own place in nature endures to attack and alter it.

In *The Reivers* we find the same festive mood of the country fair as in *A Fable* and the same journey through nature to civilization—or, as Barber traced Shakespearean comedy, "through release to clarification." In this novel, even more than in *A Fable,* the comic society triumphs. When Ned and Lucius defeat the rural constable, they do so by a retreat to another green world: "we went on to our sanctuary, where Lightning—I mean Coppermine—and the two mules stamped and swished in the dappled shade. . . ." (*Rei,* 228). Here it is possible not only to escape order by a flight to a natural sanctuary, but also to return to society and effect some change in it. Lucius returns to his grandfather; the novel ends in both a wedding and a birth; and a new order is begun. Faulkner's reading of Shakespearean comedy, so evident in the novel's frequent allusions, seems to be the basis for both this affirmation of the comic resolution and the earlier denial of that possibility. The sanctuary which had earlier been violated by anti-comic society's intrusions is finally made a source of release and clarification. Within that historic movement and this comic plot, the artist is no longer a pariah but a prophet who can accept the achievement of the past and use it to supply society with a vocabulary of salvation. The burden of Shakespeare and the influence of the past have now become the mission for the present.

Conclusion: Fiction "like *Hamlet*"

For Faulkner, Shakespeare was not merely a part of his literary environment but rather the artist who had spoken to him in his youth and whose words he remembered in his maturity. When he wrote, Faulkner remembered favorite plays, lines, and characters. Although with Murray Krieger we must perhaps admit that "in a volume centering on Shakespeare's influence . . . exaggerated claims are part of the ritual,"[51] there seems to be ample and valid evidence of Faulkner's use of these texts. He borrowed most heavily from *Macbeth, Hamlet,* and *Midsummer Night's Dream.* A graph of the number of borrowings, echoes, and allusions would reveal that Shakespeare's presence is most often felt in the first half of Faulkner's career—particularly in *Soldiers' Pay, Flags in the Dust, The Sound and the Fury,* and *Absalom, Absalom!.* Certain Shakespearean words and phrases became part of Faulkner's vocabulary in most of these and other works: "defunctive," the "dying fall," and "tomorrow, and tomorrow" appear in many of the novels and stories. And certain Shakespearean figures stand as models for Faulkner's characters: Hamlet, Macbeth, Lady Macbeth, Hotspur, Prince Hal, and Falstaff were his favorites. Occasionally he employed lines or suggested characters from many other plays and poems as well.

In New Orleans the young Faulkner boasted that "I could write a play like *Hamlet* if I wanted to." In one sense, he succeeded. He remained ever mindful of Shakespeare and *Hamlet,* and he suggested again and again the problem of competition with the past. Much as Hamlet himself was obsessed with his father's accomplishments and legacy, Faulkner's characters look to the glories of the past and lament their own lack of initiative. In this sense Bayard Sartoris, Horace Benbow, Quentin Compson, Gail Hightower, and Ike McCaslin are Faulkner's own Hamlets. After *Absalom,* and particularly with the emergence of

Gavin Stevens, his characters are more at ease with the past and with literature, but that resolution suggests in itself the importance of Shakespeare's influence on Faulkner's work.[52]

NOTES

1. James K. Feibleman, "Literary New Orleans Between World Wars," *The Southern Review,* NS 1 (1965): 705–706.

2. William Faulkner, "American Drama: Eugene O'Neill," (1922; reprinted in *William Faulkner: Early Prose and Poetry.* Carvel Collins, ed. [Boston: Little, Brown and Company, 1962]), 87. Henceforth, all references to this work will be included in the text and will be abbreviated as *EPP.*

3. William Faulkner, *Selected Letters of William Faulkner.* Joseph L. Blotner, ed. (New York: Random House, 1977), 20. Unfortunately, Blotner does not identify the story in either the notes or his *Faulkner: A Biography,* 2 vols., (New York: Random House, 1974).

4. *William Faulkner of Oxford,* ed. James W. Webb and A. Wigfall Green (Baton Rouge: Louisiana State University Press, 1965), 134.

5. Blotner, *Biography,* 500. Blotner's source for this remark is "an unpublished portion of class conference, University of Virginia, 15 May 1957." See his notes to volume 1: 500, line 18.

6. *Lion in the Garden: Interviews with William Faulkner,* ed. Michael Millgate and James B. Meriwether (New York: Random House, 1968), 276.

7. Blotner, *Biography,* 110–111.

8. Ibid., 101. *As You Like It* was also performed in Oxford during Faulkner's youth. See *Biography,* 116.

9. Ibid., 160.

10. Murry C. Falkner, *The Falkners of Mississippi: A Memoir* (Baton Rouge: Louisiana State University Press, 1967), 17.

11. Robert Coughlan, *The Private World of William Faulkner* (New York: Avon Books, 1953), 39.

12. John Faulkner, *my brother Bill: An Affectionate Reminiscence* (New York: Trident Press, 1963), 130.

13. Blotner, *Biography,* 203.

14. Ibid., 251.

15. Ibid., 251.

16. Ibid., Notes, 47.

17. *Oxford,* 134.

18. In *A Fable,* 1954, reprinted with an introduction by Michael Novak (New York: The New American Library, 1968), the aide reveals to his commander a desire similar to Shakespeare's:

"I wanted to be brave."

"Be what?" the division commander said.

"You know: a hero. Instead I made women's clothes. So I thought of becoming an actor—Henry V—Tartuffe better than nothing—even Cyrano. But that would be just acting, pretence—somebody else, not me. Then I knew what to do. Write it."

"Write it?"

"Yes. The plays. Myself write the plays, rather than just act out somebody else's idea of what is brave. Invent myself the glorious deeds and situations, create myself the people brave enough to perform and face and endure them" (59).

19. *Lion,* 49.

20. *Selected Letters*, 142.

21. *Lion*, 59–60.

22. Ibid., 238.

23. See, for example, *Faulkner in the University: Class Conferences at the University of Virginia 1957–1958*, Frederick Gwynn and Joseph Blotner, eds. (Charlottesville: University Press of Virginia, 1959), 286; *Faulkner at Nagano*, Robert A. Felliffe, ed. (Tokyo: Kenkyusha Press, 1962), 154; *Faulkner at West Point*, Joseph L. Fant and Robert Ashley, eds. (1964; reprinted by New York: Vintage Books, 1969), 114. See also interview with Cynthia Grenier in *Lion* (217).

24. Blotner, *Biography*, 1306.

25. *William Faulkner's Library: A Catalogue*, ed. Joseph Blotner (Charlottesville: University Press of Virginia, 1964), 71–72.

26. All future references to Faulkner's works will also be included in the text. The following are the editions cited and the abbreviations used:

> *William Faulkner: Early Prose and Poetry*. Comp. and introd. by Carvel Collins. Boston: Little, Brown and Co., 1962. *EPP*
>
> *Flags in the Dust*. Edited with an Introduction by Douglas Day. 1973; rpt., New York: Vintage Books, 1974. *FD*
>
> *Mosquitoes: A Novel*. 1927; rpt., New York: Liveright Publishing Corporation, n.d. *Mos*
>
> *Soldiers' Pay*. 1926; rpt., New York: Liveright, 1970. *SP*

27. Noel Polk, "William Faulkner's 'Marionettes,'" *Mississippi Quarterly* 26 (1973): 247. See also H. Edward Richardson, *William Faulkner: The Journal to Self-Discovery* (Columbia: University of Missouri Press, 1969), 57; and Blotner, *Biography*, Notes, 47.

28. Faulkner was probably introduced to Moore's work by Phil Stone. In his essay on Eugene O'Neill, Faulkner states that "some one has said—a Frenchman, probably; they have said everything—that art is preeminently provincial" (*EPP*, 86). In the preface to *The Marble Faun*, Stone correctly attributes this remark to Moore (7). In his unfinished novel *Elmer*, Faulkner mentions "the ghost of George Moore's dead life" (cited by Blotner in the *Biography*, 460). Faulkner also included a work by Moore in his library; Michael Millgate, *The Achievement of William Faulkner* (1963; reprinted by New York: Vintage Books, 1971), also feels that Moore was an important influence at this time (16).

29. Mrs. Powers and her husband "had tried to eradicate to-morrow from the world" (36; cf. 173, 181). Cecily Saunders's brother echoes the thrice-repeated tomorrow as he anticipates the sight of Donald's scar (102). Mr. Saunders puts off a troubling discussion with Rev. Mahon until "tomorrow" and again "tomorrow" (114). Jones reassures himself that "there's always to-morrow" (135). Gilligan sees blooms "waiting for tomorrow" (290). And after Donald's death, Emmy consoles herself with the fact that "to-morrow was washday" (301).

30. See Blotner, *Biography*, 423, 428; Millgate, 53; and Edmund Volpe, *A Reader's Guide to William Faulkner* (New York: Farrar, Strauss and Giroux, 1964), 50.

31. See Blotner, *Biography*, 428.

32. Joseph Brogunier, "The Jefferson Urn: Faulkner's Literary Sources and Influences," (Dissertation, U. of Minnesota, 1969), 42.

33. See Blotner, *Biography*, 512–22 and Millgate, 68, 73.

34. Blotner suggests borrowings from Eliot and similarities to Lawrence, Huxley, and Joyce (*Biography*, 514–20).

35. Richard P. Adams, *Faulkner: Myth and Motion* (Princeton: Princeton University Press, 1968), 46.

36. Brogunier, 42.

37. *Lion*, 255.

38. See Blotner, *Biography*, 532. Faulkner deleted the genealogy from *Flags in the Dust* before he submitted it to Liveright for publication in 1927. After several rejections the novel appeared in a much abbreviated fashion as *Sartoris,* the only version available

until Douglas Day edited the original text for publication in 1973. Blotner offers a brief comparison of the two texts (*Biography*, 584), as does Millgate, 76–85.

39. Laren Stevens, "*Sartoris:* Germ of the Apocalypse," *Dalhousie Review* 49 (1969): 80.

40. Blotner reports this statement made "in a highly rhetorical and sometimes illegible one and a half sheet of manuscript" (*Biography*, 531). In a review of *In April Once* by W. A. Percy, Faulkner expresses a similar lament: "Mr. Percy—like alas! how many of us—suffered the misfortune of having been born out of his time" (*EPP*, 71).

41. Millgate, 79.

42. *Essays, Speeches and Public Letters*, James B. Meriwether, ed. (New York: Random House, 1966), 145.

43. *Lion*, 239.

44. Richard P. Adams, "The Apprenticeship of William Faulkner," *Tulane Studies in English* 12 (1962): 113–56; reprinted in *William Faulkner: Four Decades of Criticism*, Linda Welshimer Wagner, ed. (East Lansing: Michigan State University Press, 1973), 14–15. See also Carvel Collins, "Faulkner's *The Sound and the Fury*," *Explicator* 17 (1958): 19, and "The Interior Monologues of *The Sound and the Fury*," *English Institute Essays 1952;* Lawrence Thompson, "Mirror Analogues in *The Sound and the Fury*," *English Institute Essays 1952;* Marjorie Ryan, "The Shakespearean Symbolism in *The Sound and the Fury*," *Faulkner Studies* 2 (1955): 40–44; Dante Cantrill, "Told by an Idiot," Dissertation, University of Washington, 1974.

45. See William Troy, "And Tomorrow," *The Nation* 140 (1935): 393; Edmund Volpe, *Reader's Guide to William Faulkner* (New York: Farrar, Strauss and Giroux, 1964), 106; Blotner, *Biography*, 872.

46. C. L. Barber, *Shakespeare's Festive Comedy* (Princeton: Princeton University Press, 1959).

47. James Mellard, "Caliban as Prospero: Benjy and *The Sound and the Fury*," *Novel* 3 (1969/1970): 233–248.

48. See Robert Slabey, "Faulkner's 'Waste Land' Vision in *Absalom, Absalom!*," *Mississippi Quarterly* 14 (1961): 153–61 and Ilse Dusoir Lind, "The Design and Meaning of *Absalom, Absalom!*," *PMLA* 70 (1955): 887–912.

49. Faulkner to Robert Haas, 8 July 1938; *Letters*, 106.

50. Ibid., 332.

51. Murray Krieger, "Shakespeare and the Critic's Idolatry of the Word," in *Shakespeare: Aspects of Influence*, G. B. Evans, ed. (Cambridge: Harvard University Press, 1976), 193.

52. For a complete discussion of Shakespeare's influence on Faulkner, see my dissertation "Shakespeare and Faulkner: A Study in Influence," Pennsylvania State University, 1978. Included is a bibliography of earlier studies, to which I should add John B. Rosenman, "Another *Othello* Echo in *As I Lay Dying*," *Notes on Mississippi Writers* 8 (1975): 19–21, and Mario L. D'Avanzo, "Love's Labors: Byron Bunch and Shakespeare," *Notes on Mississippi Writers* 10 (1977): 80–86.

Southern Formalism at Shakespeare:
Ransom on the Sonnets

Kelsie B. Harder

Shakespeare was not a non-person to the group of writers and critics that I tag here, somewhat nervously, as Southern Formalists. Still, before naming names, I recently made a haphazard check of indexes to some forty books bearing upon the works of such southerners as John Crowe Ransom, Allen Tate, Donald Davidson, Cleanth Brooks, Robert Penn Warren, as well as some others who now would be considered minor members of the Nashville Group,[1] although Walter Clyde Curry was to become a scholar of great stature and can hardly be considered minor. In many studies of these writers Shakespeare is not indexed, a shocking discovery in light of the amount of commentary upon the works of Shakespeare found in the major critical studies by Ransom, Tate, Warren, and Brooks.[2] Despite the inattention of literary historians, we can safely say, however, that Shakespeare was a most proper concern for the Nashville Group and sometimes a veritable obsession, with good reason, too. Historians aside, the matter of southern formalism needs auditing.

Before moving too far into the rituals of formalism, we need to establish that the southern writers, including the litany of the great and the lesser great, were indelibly and sometimes forcibly students of the works of Shakespeare. In the schools Shakespeare stood, like the tree of knowledge in Eden, in the center of the curriculum, the one writer to be read carefully, sometimes in slightly bowdlerized form, and memorized hardly less conscientiously. The plots had already been assimilated by the time a student entered any higher educational school, although earlier writers than John Crowe Ransom and his students—Allen Tate, Robert Penn Warren, and Cleanth Brooks—would certainly have continued their reading of Shakespeare after their formal

schooling had ended. Still, university education for Ransom, and those who followed him, made all the difference in their approach to Shakespeare's works.

A formal approach to works of art comes about through reflection, study, and generalization, conditions that demand detachment from the emotion expressed in the work being considered. A formalist critic explores facets of emotion and knowledge and tries to signify a unity, an inseparability, often exceeding the logic of the act it has unified. This unity may be inexplicable, able only to be described. This type of critic must find a point of departure, an objective correlative. The impressionist is concerned only with the id, the sensual gratification that accompanies pleasurable texts. The historian looks for diachronic transformations, often sliding directly into the "history of ideas," still a strong critical homeground for literary historians and teachers of philosophy. Others also have their particular strategies for exploring and often ransacking a text, whether it is a poem, play, novel, or short story. The formalistic critic, however, attempts to avoid the emotions of the psychological content of the text, looking for knowledge beyond the emotion, which indeed cannot be replicated in the reader but can become a part of a larger experience, recognized as knowledge.

Precisely here the formalistic critic has to formulate, to find the lever that moves the text—in a good Agrarian's terms, "find the handle." Furthermore, somewhere here is that particular brand of southernness that appears almost spontaneously in John Crowe Ransom's poetry and criticism, the recognition of metaphor as the element of detachment and as a path the poet travels to learn the infinite "ways of looking at the blackbird." One property the southerner has in abundance and multiplicity is imagery, available in the nearest hickory tree or in nature's heated and teeming lusciousness that clings to the swamps, bayous, woodlands, and fields. First, such a land existed and to an extent still exists, although the critic could prove that these landscapes have a way of shifting territories as needed. Second, the critic and writer steeped in the convoluted, intense, sometimes obscure imagery of Shakespeare could not avoid awareness of a similarity between the reality outside the bay windows and the

wildly metaphorical language gyrating from the pages of Shakespeare. The combination is still heady and no doubt was to the
educated southerner of earlier decades.

To connect the two elements of southern landscapes and
Shakespearean imagery, a cohabitation had to take place. The
reader (or critic) had to accept the bracelet of marital restraint,
with form controlling content, encircling the impulses; otherwise, romantic and promiscuous chaos would result. The
educated mind, an instrument for framing technologies out of
abstractions, had to tame excesses if any order were to be structured. A southerner like Ransom, for instance, did not recover
graciously from the exposure to both nature and Shakespeare's
texts, each seemingly disordered, erring like searching green
creepers. Out of any mass of materials the poet (here Ransom)
must search out sanity, order, and balance, refusing to allow the
imagery to suffocate them through sheer bulk and excess. Taming has to come through recognition of metaphor and its
generalization, symbol. Metaphor and symbol particularize the
"concrete" and enrich knowledge by securing image and ab-
straction. At this point Ransom exercises his greatest influence
on himself and on literature.

Ransom, who had a passion for wit and irony in both his style
and criticism, wrote in an otherwise less than distinguished essay, "Theory of Poetic Form,"[3] that he feared he "might be
ticketed in advance . . . as a 'formalistic critic,'" a label he
professed to abhor, just as he reacted to being ticketed as a "new
critic," in both instances with some justification, no matter how
disarming the style. Ransom did have difficulties with formal
criticism, and ironically he seems to have accumulated such
unofficial titles through a mirror reflection from the formalism of
his student Cleanth Brooks, whom he chided at times for being a
trifle too ingenious in searching out in poetry "some irony, some
form of 'conflict' and 'inclusions of opposites.'" Brooks, according to Ransom, had fallen under the influence of I. A.
Richards and was seeking reconciliations of opposites in poems
when such resolutions simply were not possible: ". . . when
there is no resolution we have a poem without a structural unity;
and that this is precisely the intention of irony, which therefore is

something special, and ought to be occasional."[4] This is the irony found in indecision, and, by extension, what Ransom certainly would have meant by metaphysical wit.

The passage is crucial, for within it can be detected a quality of southernness that needs describing. Irony is a key term to Ransom's understanding and interpretation both of his sectionalism and of the tragedy, as he saw it, of the recent history of the South. Further, this irony in Ransom's critical makeup found a stimulus in the tense metaphysical conceits of John Donne, whose formal metaphors—the compass in "Valediction" he cited as the perfect example—dominate the structures of his poems.

The compass image has been seized upon, as Ransom wryly notes, "by Johnson, by Eliot, by everybody" as the most appropriate and perhaps the most far-fetched metaphysical metaphor.[5] Subtle, intellectualized, it still dramatizes the two lovers and makes them individuals, and in a bit of academic punning makes them, Ransom says, "slightly eccentric" in "their brilliance as sharply-textured representations." Ransom's insight here is remarkable, even after all critical dust is settled, for he manages to show a relationship between the near-satire of such particularizations and the broad satire of Restoration and eighteenth-century authors who, according to Ransom, "felt that such poetic representations were irresponsible though interesting." The need is a balance that teeters between satire and ridiculousness, "where the general behavior of the victim (here, the lovers) is so particularized, or identified with some well-known analogous behavior so exclusively as to become ridiculous. This poetry runs a great risk."[6]

Herein we find the sensitive southerner, as Ransom claims, a man of great ancestral and dynastic loss who is slightly askew, almost running in circles, a J. Alfred Prufrock in antebellum dress, hardly understanding his own behavior in an industrial and scientific culture but sufficiently in control to recognize the seduction of sentimental and excessive emotions. This dualism sometimes leaves the southerner in a state of equilibrium, standing carefully between the spiritual world and the objective one, negotiating relationships outside of context. Such a person could develop an aesthetic creed based on recognizable form within an energetic disorder, a landscape of particulars. That such persons are self-conscious, almost ridiculous, is more reason for them to develop an ironic and self-deprecating posture in order to survive socially, financially, and economically in a culture that has, through its dependence on science, negated its tradition, its integrity, and its aesthetic resources in favor of crass materialism and its consequences for the dehumanizing process.

The metaphysical mode obviously suited Ransom's critical temper during the post-Victorian era. He believed that a "metaphysical poem is an intellectual labor," where all the intellect is active but still directed by "the presidency of imagination."[7] This abstract description of metaphysical poetry differs substantially from that of some critics, specifically that of Sir Herbert Grierson, the editor of Donne's poems who "says in many places that what Donne does is to combine intellect with passion."[8] Ransom comments that "we may shiver with apprehension lest theory, or the aesthetic of poetry perish under such a definition." He would substitute "imagination" in the Coleridgean sense in place of "passion" and maintains that metaphysical poets, who also have feelings, are "self-conscious and deliberate," and, to paraphrase Ransom slightly, objectify their feelings "imaginatively into external actions," into perhaps short lyric poems nothing like the scale of a play, say, by Shakespeare, where the imagination of a lover must be subservient to the action and therefore suspect. The metaphysical poem, then, is a precise and technical definition of a feeling that has been modified by intellect and imagination, with the latter directing traffic through the structure.

This is not to say that Shakespeare did not write passages that had metaphysical elements, for according to Cleanth Brooks he obviously "in the beginning was not too far removed from Donne," as many examples from the early plays and poems, as well as from some sonnets, attest.[10] The crux of this argument, however, is that Shakespeare was "rarely willing to abandon his feelings," his looseness of subjectivity, for the imaginative rein. The pure metaphysical poet elects an image that will determine the results of feelings, as does the compass image already cited. He risks "the consequences of his own imagination," something that Shakespeare, for whatever reasons, did not allow. Ransom says, "He censored these consequences, to give them sweetness, to give them dignity; he would go a little way with one figure, usually a reputable one, then anticipate the consequences, or the best of them to take up another figure."[11]

Ransom, then, had bases from which to throw "a few stones at Shakespeare, aiming them as accurately as" he could "at the vulnerable parts."[12] To be sure, no razing could take place, "for Shakespeare is an institution as well established as the industrial revolution, or the Protestant churches."[13] Limiting his remarks to the sonnets, Ransom examines the quality of Shakespeare's poetry by contrasting it with the metaphysical mode, a yardstick that for some critics may not quite measure the yard.[14] But the inspector must perform his duty and does so within the specifications.

Ransom begins his inspection by citing Shakespeare for poor construction. About half of the sonnets, he points out, fall short of being each "three co-ordinate quatrains and then a couplet which will relate to the series collectively."[15] Each quatrain must permit one image applicable to the theme, with the concluding couplet a summation and reconciliation, a determination. Ransom finds few well-built Shakespearean sonnets; number 87, "Farewell! thou art too dear for my possessing," is the only one perfectly built, he argues, although others manage to stay within the imagistic requirements of the quatrain despite their defects in balance and climax. Specifically, Shakespeare had trouble remaining within limits; his feelings sprouted into diverse images which become plants of exceptional and luxuriant growth, out of control of the gardener. The sonnet form was simply too small to hold Shakespeare's imagery. He had to have room for the emotions to expand, to overflow, to swell, maybe to fester. The fourteen-line structure, with its rigid demands for tension and balance, was not the place for the excesses of a romantic; hence, says Ransom, Shakespeare was not good at lyric poetry where feelings must be directed into a controlled imaginative event. On the other hand, Shakespeare's mind may have been incapable of externalizing any logical order outside the dramatic context, despite the formalist's attempts to show "psychological" connectors between the seemingly discontinuous images in selected passages from Shakespeare's plays.[16]

Others in the Nashville Group never attacked Shakespeare's poetry in quite the same way, and some tried to mitigate some of Ransom's insistency on strict and rigorous formalism in looking at the sonnets.[17] Allen Tate, a close friend but never really a disciple of Ransom, claims that the essay on the sonnets contains "valuable insights into the operation of the metaphysical 'conceit'" but that Ransom's "rejection of Shakespeare's sonnets seems to be a result of deductive necessity in his premises, or the courage of mere logic; . . ."[18] Cleanth Brooks, in some ways a more formal critic than Ransom, tends to agree that Donne is "a better lyric poet than Shakespeare because Donne's images 'work out.'" Nevertheless, he is "inclined to feel that Ransom demands that all images work out as Donne's more 'logical images work out; . . .'" This to Brooks seems "to elevate one admirable strategy into the whole art."[19] The comment is telling, and places Ransom's strictures in perspective without denying their validity.

In *Understanding Poetry*,[20] Cleanth Brooks and Robert Penn Warren follow closely the dictates of Ransom, in that selections, commentary, and suggested exercises center on form and content of poems rather than on literary history and impressions. The approach is formal and linguistic and attends the literary work.[21] Warren, aside from his pedagogical texts, admits that Shakespeare was the author who had the greatest influence on his poetry and fiction.[22] Brooks never attempts a close analysis of Shakespedare's sonnets and lyric poetry, but his analyses of passages in the plays follows the formalist's "articles."

The southern quality in Ransom's approach to Shakespeare does not easily surface, since southernness is often associated with romantic excess, sentimentality, outmoded honor, hot-tempered violence, and racism. Ransom rebelled against these features as they are portrayed in literature. The reasons for such rebellion perhaps should be left better to the biographer or psycho-historian. In the case of Ransom, not only is his aesthetic sensibility grounded in the form and imagery ("structure" and "texture") of the landscape, but it is also cognitive, that is, knowledgeable and recursive, both human characteristics that promote mental balance. In this sensibility occurs a need for confrontation with specific moral problems involving life and death, although, as Brooks points out, "the purpose of literature is not to point a moral."

Ransom saw the southern way of life as one that demanded responsibility and order with "a considerable disorder or deformation," these to test the mettle of the human being. It was (to Ransom) one that in the past allowed an individual to pit himself against and with God and nature without being overwhelmed by either. This balance, he believed, gives form to existence and by extension to art without dehumanizing. Otherwise, excesses will occur to such an extent as to force irrationality into contention with order. Art, then, he felt, can become a way of structuring and strengthening life.

In Donne's lyrics Ransom found detachment, irony, and emotional control, qualities he missed in Shakespeare's sonnets, where he felt the poet over-sentimentalized the relationship between himself and the lover or lovers and indulged in a whining and evasive self-pity. Missing from the sonnets, Ransom said, is a capacity for reflection, for understanding the totality of man's experience. Another way of putting it, without over-elaboration, is that Shakespeare was not an Agrarian. Conscious of the loss the South had experienced after the Civil War, Ransom rejected the easy romantic path of acceptance of the modern age through science, progress, and over-simplification. Above all he had an obsessive distrust of the romantic mind that too often encompassed these features. Shakespeare's sonnets illustrated such poetic weaknesses and as art suffered accordingly.

Strictures on the sonnets were not Ransom's only concerns in his discussion of aspects of Shakespeare's work. He held in common with other southern intellectuals a strong respect for rhetoric, a stance that controlled many areas of southern life such as speech, government, religion, and poetic artifice. Three members of the Nashville Group—Davidson, Brooks, and Warren—wrote successful college textbooks on rhetoric, in each instance reflecting traditional, classical, and demanding views. William Wimsatt and Cleanth Brooks, for instance, argue that "rhetoric is a powerful form of incitation and subdual; it works with an armory of flashing devices."[23] Rhetoric—divested of its classical luggage of invention, disposition, and memory, but still carrying elocution and delivery—becomes style, with "easy ornament" reduced in order to emphasize the practical. While not accepting completely the consequences, which were indeed far-ranging, Brooks and Wimsatt clearly show that certain tropes, metaphor and irony, are useful in a technological sense.[24]

Ransom nowhere suggests that he instilled such resolute opinions in Brooks, his student, but he did help to mold his style. One of Ransom's more often reprinted essays, "On Shakespeare's Language,"[25] has been slighted as a statement of praise, a gesture toward reconciliation with Shakespeare's style or styles, or maybe the Bard's lack of a stability of language. Ransom centers on Shakespeare's bilingual style, the mixing of Latinity and the vernacular, citing as examples phrases such as: "The multitudinous seas incarnadine," "Absent thee from felicity awhile," "That thou mayst shake the superflux to them," and "blue promontory." Shakespeare compounded Latinical elements differently from his contemporaries and long after earlier writers had consciously Latinized their texts. Ransom slyly suggests that Shakespeare was behind the times in style, retaining strategies of poetic devices long after they had fallen into disuse.

Shakespeare also must have learned enough Latin in grammar school to acquire a fondness for it, never making it a part of his language but using it as a foreign language that has not been quite mastered but is still available for special placements, just as some writers today drop a French or German expression into an otherwise straight English text. Such actions would appear, to Ransom, a display of "vulgar affectation." The Latinical practices occur in the later, mature Shakespearean plays, adding to Ransom's thesis that Shakespeare consciously inserted the Latinisms, equally conscious of their foreignness, to be deliberately bilingual. Not only can bilingualism be found in set pieces in the dramas, but it also permeates the sonnets, especially the later ones where Shakespeare seems to have updated the grammar school practice of coupling languages as a part of the teaching enterprise. He concludes that Shakespeare had a certain preoccupation with the Latinity in the sonnets. He never quite says that this tendency is a regression in the poet's faculties.

Of course, such a formalistic critique of Shakespeare's sonnets cannot be said to have damaged the reputation of the dramatist, nor was that Ransom's ostensible intention, for popular reaction and crystalized tradition are not easily persuaded to accept the dismantling of a beautified structure, whatever the condition of the architecture. Ransom was no giant killer, but he could be a gadfly. Critics, however, certainly are now more aware of problems of structure and composition not only in Shakespeare's sonnets but also in the lyrics of others of lesser stature. In addition, they surely are better readers of Shakespeare if only because they are forced to give a rationale for defending the sonnets.

NOTES

1. I prefer here to use the term Nashville Group rather than the Fugitives or the Agrarians, since not all contributed to both groups. For instance, Cleanth Brooks was not one of the original Fugitives, being a few years too young. *The Fugitive* ceased publication in 1925, the date Brooks entered Vanderbilt University.

2. John L. Stewart, *The Burden of Time* (Princeton: University Press, 1965) omits the name of Shakespeare from his index but mentions him and some of his works in passing. Louise Cowen, *The Fugitive Group: A Literary History* (Baton Rouge: Louisiana State University Press, 1959); Louis D. Rubin, Jr., *The Wary Fugitives: Four Poets and the South* (Baton Rouge: Louisiana State University Press, 1978); and William J. Handy, *Kant and the Southern New Critics* (Austin: University of Texas Press, 1963) make no reference to Shakespeare. Alexander Karanikas, *Tillers of a Myth: Southern Agrarians as Social and Literary Critics* (Madison: The University of Wisconsin Press, 1969), includes one reference, but again only in a general comment.

3. John Crowe Ransom, "Theory of Poetic Form," in *A Symposium on Formalist Criticism* (Austin: The Humanities Research Center, the University of Texas, 1965), 14–25, reprinted from *The Texas Quarterly*. Others appearing in *A Symposium* are Mark Schorer, Elder Olson, Eliseo Vivas, and Kenneth Burke.

4. Ibid.

5. Ransom, ibid., p. 189, quotes the relevant portion of Donne's "Valediction":

> If they be two, they are two so
> As stiff twin compasses are two;
> Thy soul, the fixed foot, makes no show
> To move, but doth if the other do.
>
> And though it in the center sit,
> Yet when the other far doth roam,
> It leans and hearkens after it,
> And grows erect as that comes home.
>
> Such wilt thouh be to me, who must,
> Like the other foot, obliquely run;

> Thy firmness makes my circle just,
> And makes me end where I begun.

6. Ibid., 190.

7. John Crowe Ransom, *The World's Body* (Baton Rouge: Louisiana University Press, 1968), 292.

8. Ibid., 289.

9. Ibid., 289–91.

10. Cleanth Brooks, *The Well Wrought Urn* (New York: Harcourt Brace, 1947), 24.

11. Ransom, *The World's Body*, 287.

12. "Shakespeare at Sonnets," in ibid., 270.

13. Ibid.

14. See in particular the strictures noted in Albert C. Baugh, ed., *A Literary History of England* (New York: Appleton–Century–Crofts, 1948, 1967), 631–636; also, Thornton H. Parsons, *John Crowe Ransom* (New York: Twayne Publishers, Inc., 1969), who praises Ransom for contributing eleven poems "to the permanent tradition of English and American poetry," but nevertheless catalogues Ransom's weaknesses and "fussy eccentricities: his addition to archaism and nostalgia, to innocuous drollery, to grandiloquence, to an anti-Victorian toughness, to flaccid iron," all of which Parsons says derive from Ransom's fierce self-control of any emotionalism.

15. Ransom, "Shakespeare at Sonnets," 273.

16. Brooks, *The Well Wrought Urn*, 245–246.

17. Ibid., 243–244. See also Allen Tate, *On the Limits of Poetry* (New York: The Swallow Press and William Morrow & Company, 1948), pp. 79–80.

18. Allen Tate, *On the Limits of Poetry*, 79, footnote 1.

19. Brooks, *The Well Wrought Urn*, 243–244.

20. Cleanth Brooks and Robert Penn Warren, *Understanding Poetry* (New York: Holt, Rinehart and Winston, 1938, 1950, 1960, 1976).

21. See Cleanth Brooks, "The Uses of Formal Analysis," in Gerald J. Goldberg and Nancy M. Goldberg, eds., *The Modern Critical Spectrum* (Englewood Cliffs, N.J.: Prentice-Hall, 1962), reprinted from *The Kenyon Review* (1951), in which Brooks lists the "articles of faith" of formalistic criticism to which he subscribes. Without denigrating Brooks's refining, one can find all the "articles" scattered through the critical commentaries by Ransom.

22. Charles H. Bohner, *Robert Penn Warren* (New York: Twayne Publishers, Inc., 1964), 160.

23. William K. Wimsatt, Jr. and Cleanth Brooks, *Literary Criticism: A Short History* (New York: Random House, 1957), 143.

24. Ibid., 222–26, *passim*.

25. *John Crowe Ransom: Poems and Essays* (New York: Alfred A. Knopf, 1955), 118–135; and the Goldbergs' *The Modern Critical Spectrum*, 48–57.

Renaissance Men:
Shakespeare's Influence on Robert Penn Warren

Mark Royden Winchell

The study of literary influence is fraught with pitfalls. One can follow the path of what Gore Vidal calls the "scholar squirrel" and get caught up in the cataloging of adventitious parallels and pointless verbal echoes, or one can indulge in the sort of cryptic psycho-criticism which Harold Bloom has recently popularized. The problem becomes even more acute when dealing with Shakespeare, because it is arguable that within the past three and a half centuries those English-speaking writers who have *not* been influenced by the Venerable Bard are in a minority. With Robert Penn Warren, however, we have a case where the study of Shakespeare's influence can be a useful critical tool.

When we think of Warren we are apt to think of the author of *All the King's Men;* of one of the most important poets of the past sixty years; of the editor, textbook author, and seminal literary critic. But we must also remember that Warren has spent almost his entire adult life as an academic. And from his early days as a Rhodes Scholar at Oxford to his more recent years as a professor at Yale, his primary teaching interest has been in the literature of the English Renaissance. In a 1978 interview he maintained that the most satisfying courses he had ever given were seminars in "Elizabethan literature, Renaissance, and Shakespeare."[1] Elsewhere, he has acknowledged Shakespeare as the single greatest influence on his writing.[2]

Given such external evidence, it is reasonable to assume that a study of Warren's use of Shakespeare would shed some light on his own work. Before examining the connection between their creative efforts, however, we might do well to consider Warren's critical comments about Shakespeare. Not only do those comments illuminate Shakespeare's writings, but they also suggest standards by which to judge Warren's fiction and verse.[3]

A Critique of Pure Poetry

One conclusion which we can draw about Robert Penn Warren on the basis of his response to Shakespeare is that Warren's own critical sensibility frequently differed from that of his mentor, John Crowe Ransom. It has been too widely assumed that the Vanderbilt New Critics were a sort of literary Mafia with Ransom as amiable godfather and Warren and Cleanth Brooks as eager young hit men. To see that this was in fact not the case, we need only consider the controversy which arose when Ransom submitted his essay "Shakespeare at Sonnets" to Brooks and Warren at the *Southern Review.*

In his cover letter to this essay, Ransom notes—a bit defensively—"I am being a little rough on Shakespeare in a magazine edited by two great Shakespeareans."[4] Although the response of these two great Shakespeareans has not been preserved, one can infer its general drift from a letter which Ransom wrote to Allen Tate shortly thereafter: "The boys deal pretty pedantically with my poor paper. . . . I really stepped on their toes a little come to think about it. For Red [Warren] is a Shakespearean and would not like my irresponsible knocks for the comfort of the Philistines" ("Divergence," 171).

Ransom's essay compares Shakespeare's sonnets unfavorably with those of John Donne. Because Ransom sees poetry as a melding of metrical structure with a paraphrasable prose content, he tends to place great stress on the *logical* development of imagery and to abjure poetic associations which are primarily emotional. As a result, he sees Shakespeare's poetry as being the precursor of some of the more baneful aspects of Romanticism.

If one grants Ransom's critical prescriptions, his essay is remarkably consistent and persuasive. In summarizing the argument of that essay, Thomas Daniel Young notes:

Shakespeare wrote in the sonnets an "associationist poetry," one that is "rich and suggestive even while it is vague and cloudy." In this kind of verse the "pretty words have pleasing if indefinite associations," and because the "associations tend rather to cohere than to repel each other" it appears to be a poetry of "wonderful precision, when logically it is a poetry of wonderful imprecision." The violence of syntax, as well as that of imagery, in Shakespeare's poetry often results in obscurity, making it resist paraphrase and destroying its structural integrity.[5]

Warren and Brooks respond much more favorably to Shakespeare's poetry because they reject the implicit dualism of Ransom's aesthetics. They see logical content as being an important ingredient in much fine poetry, but not as an indispensable element of all verse. For them, the dramatic situation in which a poem is framed can create a context in which illogical associations are eminently valid. This is evident from their discussion of "Cleopatra's Lament"[6] in their widely used textbook-anthology *Understanding Poetry*.[7]

The editors begin by reminding their reader of the circumstances in which this speech is delivered. With Antony recently dead, Cleopatra is now at the mercy of the conquering Octavius. As Octavius's emissary Dolabella seeks to arrange the terms of Cleopatra's surrender, the Egyptian queen remembers the days of her former happiness with Antony. "I dreamed there was an Emperor Antony," she begins, and her entire speech is couched in dream imagery which paints a picture of Antony "in shocking contrast to what any human being might be" (Brooks and Warren, 291).

Brooks and Warren continue:

> Cleopatra starts with a comparison so extreme as to break any ordinary logic—Antony's face as the very heavens, with eyes like sun and moon lighting the little earth. But the violation of logic is an index to the force of feeling that now breaks out. We feel a dramatic grounding for the violence and elevation of the utterance—with its sense of dreamlike release and apocalyptic grandeur—which is not unlike the language of, say, the Book of Revelations, another attempt to utter the unutterable. (291)

(The speech in question is not a soliloquy, of course, but part of a dialogue with Dolabella who represents the voice of realism and whose attempts to break in on Cleopatra's revery help to create dramatic tension in the scene.)

In the second section of her speech, Cleopatra appears to be attempting a systematic description of Antony. But, as Brooks and Warren point out, "this systematic description breaks into a series of images which have no consistent relation to the main image with which the passage begins" (291). Far from finding this lack of systematic coherence to be a poetic flaw, Brooks and Warren see it as yet another index of the dramatic urgency of the situation.

The aesthetic principles of *Understanding Poetry* are much broader and more inclusive than Ransom's.[8] Whereas Ransom believed that, unless it were rigorously shaped by logic, feeling had no place in poetry, Brooks and Warren are much more willing to accept feeling as being itself a shaping agent. For this reason, they defend Shakespeare's use of mixed metaphor as dramatically appropriate to "Cleopatra's Lament." Indeed, consistent development of imagery and metaphor would seem—in this context—sterile, artificial, and psychologically implausible. Cleopatra's speech is quite properly a poetry of *discontinuity.* Shakespeare has not sought to write metaphysical verse and failed. Rather, he has attempted and achieved totally different, but equally valid, poetic ends.

Warren's views on the nature of poetry are most fully articulated in his 1942 essay "Pure and Impure Poetry." Although we cannot be certain why he chose this particular title, we do know that the distinction between dramatic poetry and lyric, or "pure," poetry had been made by Ransom four years earlier in "Shakespeare at Sonnets." In his essay Warren takes an approach toward poetic theory that is much more eclectic than Ransom's and even cautions against the limitations of critical strategies and labels. Warren writes:

> Poetry wants to be pure, but poems do not. At least, most of them do not want to be too pure. . . . They mar themselves with cacophanies, jagged rhythms, ugly words and ugly thoughts, colloquialisms, cliches, sterile technical terms, headwork and argument, self-contradictions, clevernesses, irony, realism—all things which call us back to the world of prose and imperfection.[9]

Warren illustrates his point by referring to a scene which, on the surface, appears to be pure and lyrical—the balcony scene from *Romeo and Juliet.* Here we seem to have the spiritualized essence of young love, unsoiled by the dross of everyday life. But Warren reminds us that "beyond the garden wall strolls Mercutio. . . ., who is always aware that nature has other names as well as the names the pure poets and pure lovers put upon her" (6).

If the presence of a bawdy wit such as Mercutio beyond the garden wall were not harmful enough to the "purity" of this scene, we find prosaic elements introduced within the garden itself. When Romeo swears his love by the moon, Juliet replies: "O! swear not by the moon, the inconstant moon,/That monthly changes in her circled orb." In effect, she challenges Romeo's "pure poem" by questioning the aptness of his metaphor, thus injecting "the impurity of an intellectual style" into the scene (Warren, 7). Warren also notes that, within the house, we have Juliet's nurse: "the voice of expediency, of half-measures, of the view that circumstances alter cases—the voice of prose and imperfection" (p. 7).

Warren concludes that the garden scene would not have been more effective had Mercutio and the nurse been farther removed or had Juliet been more sympathetic to her lover's choice of metaphor. "The effect might even be more vulnerable poetically if the impurities were purged away. Mercutio, the lady, and the nurse are critics of the lover, who believes in pure poems, but perhaps they are necessary. Perhaps the lover can be accepted only in their context. . . . The poetry arises from a recalcitrant and contradictory context; and finally involves that context" (7).

The most extensive critical observations that Warren has written about Shakespeare are—technically speaking—not his at all but those of Slim Sarrett, a character in Warren's second novel, *At Heaven's Gate.* Obviously, we cannot take these observations at face value: Sarrett is a character in a novel, and one who is far from embodying a moral norm. It is significant, however, that Warren has inserted in almost the exact middle of his novel nearly three pages of fairly sophisticated Shakespearean criticism. By examining Sarrett's insights in relation to the novel in which they are contained, we can better understand *At Heaven's*

Gate, as well as some of the primary themes of Warren's other fictional and poetic narratives.

To begin with, Sarrett argues that one ought not to make facile assumptions about Shakespeare's moral and philosophical views based solely on the action of his plays. All intelligent critics are wary of accepting the statements made in a drama as "content-absolutes." Such critics rightly note: " 'Because Lear says so-and-so, I am not to infer that Shakespeare meant so-and-so; we must remember that Lear is a character in a play.' "[10] Unfortunately, these same critics do frequently assume that character and plot are content-absolutes. They infer "from what happens to Richard III that Shakespeare believed in and depicted a universe operating according to a moral order" (195). Such an assumption, however, is unwarranted.

Sarrett cites counter-examples to show that the moral order in Shakespeare's plays is not always consistent: "the [simplistic moral] critic forgets, or blandly neglects, the tissue of negative instances surrounding the central character—good men brought to ruin, etc.—ah, where are the pretty little princes in the Tower?" (195). Although Shakespeare may never have "painted vice as prosperous. . . ., he did something far more reprehensible; he painted virtue brought to misery" (195).

The problem with moral critics is not so much that they misread Shakespeare's plays, Sarrett argues, but that they misdirect the focus of their reading. For Shakespeare, "the tortured residuum of the Christian tradition. . . . is simply part of the stuff available—like Plutarch or Holinshed or Marlowe's mighty line or the condition of language" (195). Such elements, in other words, are the materials with which Shakespeare worked, but they are not themselves the end-product of that work.

What is of supreme importance to Shakespearean tragedy is the central theme to which all of the constituent elements of that tragedy are subservient: the necessity for self-knowledge. According to Sarrett:

The tragic flaw in the Shakespearean hero is a defect in self-knowledge. . . . Bacon wrote: Knowledge is power. Bacon was thinking of knowledge of the mechanisms of the external world. Shakespeare wrote: Self-knowledge is power. Shakespeare was thinking of the mechanisms of the spirit, to which the mechanisms of the external world, including other persons, are instruments. (196)

Although Shakespeare was interested in the success which comes with self-knowledge, "his tragedy is concerned with failure. . . . The successful man . . . offers only the smooth surface, like an egg. In so far as he is truly successful, he has no story. He is pure. But poetry is concerned with failure, distortion, imbalance—with impurity. And poetry itself is impurity" (196).

If we consider the entire context of Warren's novel, we can see that his characters—like Shakespeare's—almost all suffer from deficient self-knowledge. Although such a condition is common to much of humanity and is not a *peculiarly* Shakespearean concern, Warren's literary preoccupation with the theme of self-knowledge can be traced—at least in part—to his study of Shakespeare. Indeed, Sarrett's seminar paper is derived practically verbatim from the lectures on Shakespeare which Warren's fellow Fugitive poet Walter Clyde Curry delivered at Vanderbilt.[11]

One of the crowning ironies of *At Heaven's Gate* is the fact that Slim Sarrett can deliver such a perceptive discourse on self-knowledge in Shakespeare and yet fail to realize that he, too, is living a lie. Although able to unmask and analyze his friends with an almost voyeuristic detachment, he is himself eventually revealed as a bisexual poseur. He has manufactured a romantic past, in which his father is a riverboat captain and his mother a prostitute rather than the bland middle-class folk which they actually are, and has disguised his sexual ambivalence by taking Sue Murdoch as his mistress and devoting himself to boxing.

Although Warren's novel is more greatly influenced by Dante[12] than by Shakespeare, we can find a few affinities with the latter's work that go beyond those suggested in the critical musings of Slim Sarrett. To begin with, the novel's principal female character Sue Murdoch is an actress who plays Cordelia in an amateur production of *King Lear.* Although her acting is more than competent, Sue is incapable of analyzing the character she portrays.

Indeed, her relationship with her own father, Began Murdoch, is a perversion of that of Lear and Cordelia. Sue banishes herself from her doting father more in petulant rebellion than in moral steadfastness. And Bogan, who lacks any of Lear's virtues, resembles Shakespeare's king only in being a socially prominent man who is brought to ruin.

If we continue to search for perverse parodies of Shakespeare in *At Heaven's Gate,* we might find a suggestion of the Romeo and Juliet story in Sue Murdoch's romance with Jason Sweetwater, the labor leader who challenges Bogan Murdoch's business empire. Finally, in the wisecracking, choric figure Duckfoot Blake—who enjoys privileged status as a sort of court jester in Murdoch's firm—one could even see an updated version of the Shakespearean fool. If the other characters in Warren's novel demonstrate the limits of Baconian knowledge and power, Blake rises above their follies, disdaining with a hard-boiled cynicism the "mechanisms of the external world."

Nature's Lamp

True to his critical principles, Warren has written poetry that frequently mars itself with cacophanies, jagged rhythms, colloquialisms, irony, realism, and other things which call us back to the world of prose and imperfection. As Louis D. Rubin, Jr. has noted, Warren's imaginative work eschews the lapidary smoothness for which Ransom and Tate so assiduously strived.[13] This is not because of careless craftsmanship so much as conscious intention. A living and inclusive poetry is, by definition, impure. Accordingly, some of Warren's most representative work is characterized by the sort of emotional extravagance and violent imagery that Ransom found so objectionable in Shakespeare.

Essentially, Ransom possessed a classical temperament. For him order, regularity, logic, and symmetry were of prime importance. Warren, however, is fundamentally a modernist and a Romantic. For him discontinuity, individuality, psychology, and distortion tend more frequently to hold sway. Yet to argue that the example of Shakespeare has significantly influenced Warren's poetry, we must do more than assert the truism that Shakespeare was the literary grandfather of Romanticism and that

every quasi-Romantic writer who has come along since somehow has worked in his shadow; we must find the distinctively
Shakespearean imprint on Warren's verse. And to do that we
must return to the work of his apprenticeship.

The poetry which Warren wrote during the first twenty years
of his career is relatively closed and formal in structure and often
suggests Elizabethan models. (After the period of this early
work, there is an eleven-year gap in Warren's *Selected Poems*—
1943 to 1954—followed by the more open and personal verse of
his later years.) In a single volume from that period—*Eleven
Poems on the Same Theme* (1942)—the influence of Shakespeare
is most noticeable.

One of the eleven poems, "Terror," depicts the spiritually
catatonic modern man whose inability to formulate an "adequate
definition of terror"[14] causes him to seek ever more lurid dangers
and thrills. Such an individual is unable to "heed the criminal
king, who paints the air/With discoursed madness and pro-
truding eye" (286). This "criminal king" is Macbeth[15] and modern
man's inability to share his sense of terror reflects the banality of
our present age. Like Eliot, Warren uses analogies from our
historical as well as our literary past to shed light on the here and
now.

Elsewhere in *Eleven Poems* we find "Revelation," a psychologically acute rendering of a boy's traumatic sense of guilt at
having spoken harshly to his mother. In the course of that poem,
the boy imagines all of nature to be profoundly altered by his
deed:

When Sulla smote and Rome was racked, Augustine
Recalled how Nature, shuddering, tore her gown,
And kind changed kind, and the blunt herbivorous tooth dripped blood;
At Duncan's death, at Dunsinane, chimneys blew down.

(301)

But since his mother "was kinder than ever Rome/Dearer than
Duncan" (301), the cosmic ramifications of this lad's sin are
correspondingly more horrible. Because of the obviously ironic

tone of this poem, Warren's use of Shakespeare here is essentially mock-heroic.

Finally, we come to "Love's Parable"—a rich, bold, metaphysical poem in which a number of readers have seen traces of Shakespeare's influence. John L. Stewart, for example, after noting some parallels between Warren's poetic strategies and those of Donne, goes on to say:

> The diction and the other images show that Shakespeare, particularly through his sonnets, was a more important agent in Warren's imagination. The poem could have been written only by one who had steeped himself in Shakespeare's works. The strength of Warren's affinity for that work is suggested by the images of morbid conditions of the flesh. . . . Like Shakespeare, Warren was obsessed with the canker rotting the substance beneath the winsome surface, and henceforth he used some form of that metaphor many times in his works to suggest a secret evil within the most innocent seeming occasion.[16]

In the ten stanzas of this poem Warren writes of the failure of a love affair, but instead of giving us the mimetic particulars of the situation he piles one elaborate simile on top of another. Although some of these similes remind one of Donne, Warren's refusal to follow any of them through in an extended and systematic way is more characteristic of Shakespeare. At various points in the poem, the relationship of the lovers is compared to that of: a conquered people and a benevolent despot, two suns, and iron and a magnet; while their misfortune calls to mind the fate of: "blockhead masons" who tear down ancient monuments to build their hovels, a "wastrel bankrupt," victims of an infectious disease, and a "pest-bit whore."

As Stewart has indicated, Warren's fondness for images of rotting flesh is also vintage Shakespeare. Consider, for example, the following lines:

> But we have seen the fungus eyes
> Of misery spore in the night,
> And marked, of friends, the malices
> That stain, like smoke, the day's fond light,

And marked how ripe injustice flows,
How ulcerous, how acid, then
How flesh on the sounder grows
Till rot engross the estate of men;

And marked within, the inward sore
Of self that cankers at the bone . . .

(312–313)

During the eleven-year hiatus in his *Selected Poems* Warren published two novels, two volumes of short stories, and *Brother to Dragons,* a book-length "Tale in Verse and Voices."[17] This latter work is regarded by many readers as its author's poetic masterpiece, and it clearly marks a departure from the Fugitive verse of Warren's early career. Moreover, from both a thematic and a technical standpoint, it suggests aspects of Shakespearean influence found nowhere else in Warren's poetry.

The story of *Brother to Dragons* is based loosely on a grotesque incident in the lives of Thomas Jefferson's nephews Lilburn and Isham Lewis. "On the night of December 15, 1811," Warren writes in his Foreword, "—the night when the New Madrid earthquake first struck the Mississippi Valley—Lilburn, with the assistance of Isham and in the presence of his Negroes, butchered a slave named George, whose offense had been to break a pitcher prized by" Lilburn's dead mother Lucy Jefferson Lewis.[18] Since there is no historical record of Jefferson's reaction to his nephews' brutality, Warren has created an imaginative one in a poetic dialogue which transpires at "No place" and in "Any time."

In a discussion of the use of history in Warren's fiction, L. Hugh Moore, Jr. makes an observation which is germane to *Brother to Dragons.* "Just as a comparison of Shakespeare's plays with their sources in Holinshed and elsewhere reveals the magnitude of his imagination," Moore writes, "a comparison of Warren's novels with their sources merely makes one realize the greatness of his achievement."[19] Like Shakespeare, Warren is interested less in historical facts than in the timeless truths derived from a study of the past.

To be sure, countless writers other than Warren and Shakespeare have reconstituted historical events for paradigmatic purposes. Moreover, the theme of self-knowledge, which is central to *Brother to Dragons* and which Warren has identified as the key motif in Shakespeare's plays, is so widespread as to be a nearly universal concern of the literary artist. Nor can one even claim that the nexus between historical drama and domestic tragedy is unique to Warren and Shakespeare.[20] Rather, what is crucial here is the form in which Warren has cast his poetic narrative.

Strictly speaking, *Brother to Dragons* is not a drama;[21] however, as a dialogue among sharply defined characters, it possesses dramatic qualities. In addition, that "dialogue" is only in part a conversation; its extended speeches resemble nothing so much as the introspective reflections found in Shakespearean soliloquies. Finally, the poetry itself is written in blank verse which contains, in the words of Randall Jarrell, "conscious echoes of . . . Shakespeare."[22]

When we consider the poetry that Warren has written during the past quarter-century, we do not find the accumulation of undeveloped similes and the archaic diction of "Love's Parable" or the blank-verse drama of *Brother to Dragons*.[23] We find instead other influences and the emergence of an increasingly distinctive poetic voice. Still, it is clear that for three decades Warren's poetry owed much to the fact that its author was indeed what Ransom accused him of being—a "great Shakespearean."

Fathers and Sons

Although Warren's poetry over the years has been more consistently impressive than his fiction, he is still best known to the public as the author of *All the King's Men*. One of the great novels of American literature, this book tells the story of Jack Burden, a young newspaper reporter who undergoes a profound spiritual transformation while witnessing the rise and fall of a complex, demagogic politician named Willie Stark. Stark himself, in addition to his obvious resemblance to Louisiana's legendary Huey P. Long, calls to mind recognizable Elizabethan antecedents.

To begin with, *All the King's Men* was not originally a novel at all, but a verse play called *Proud Flesh*. In speaking of his initial conception of this work, Warren invokes Shakespeare's *Julius Caesar* by referring to the assassin of his politician as a "self-appointed Brutus."[24] Elsewhere, he notes that "Huey Long and Julius Caesar both got killed in the capitol" and that he himself was teaching Shakespeare in Louisiana at the time of Long's death.[25] (There is even an element of Spenser's influence in the fact that the character in *Proud Flesh* who would later become Willie Stark was named Willie "Talos," after the "iron groom" in *The Faerie Queen.*)

Essentially, however, Willie Stark is a unique creation, not a fictionalized Huey Long or an updated Julius Caesar. Thus, when we try to push any analogy between Stark and other figures—historical or literary—too far, that analogy breaks down. Rather than being cloned from a single source, Stark's personality more closely resembles a mosaic of influences. Indeed, one can see in him as much of Brutus as of Caesar.

Like Brutus, Willie starts out as an idealist who rises to power by displacing a regime which he perceives to be unjust (albeit Stark's triumph is the bloodless one of electoral victory). Also like Brutus, Stark is initially recruited by conspirators who believe that his assistance will aid their cause. In addition, we see that increasing political involvement destroys the marriages of both men. Finally, both Stark and Brutus are undone by their attempts to achieve good ends through evil means.

The recognition that Willie Stark's story is rooted, at least in part, in Warren's knowledge of Elizabethan tragedy helps supply a needed corrective to some superficial misreadings of that story. Because of Stark's similarity to Huey Long, many early reviews of *All the King's Men* were less discussions of the novel than arguments about Long himself. As Robert B. Heilman points out, the authors of such reviews were so obsessed with topicality that they seemed incapable of reading tragedy. "One may doubt whether *Macbeth* would have been improved," Heilman continues, "if it had been conceived as a recipe for the curtailment of royal abuses."[26]

Even those persons who are perceptive enough to realize that Willie Stark is more than a thinly disguised Huey Long sometimes make the mistake of reading *All the King's Men* as a solely political novel. Such a reading, however, raises more questions than it answers. We must wonder, for example, why the domestic conflicts of Jack Burden's life play such a large role in another man's story. If Warren is concerned primarily with Willie Stark, then much of what we learn about Jack is peripheral and irrelevant. For this reason, critics who find *All the King's Men* to be an artistic success tend to regard Burden not as a mere Conradian narrator but as the novel's central character. For that reason, the most intriguing Shakespearean analogue for us to consider may not be *Julius Caesar* but *Hamlet.*

The Hamlet story would have had obvious appeal for a southern American writer of Warren's generation. As Leslie Fiedler maintains in his essay "Caliban or Hamlet: A Study in Literary Anthropology," the Hamlet image "has most obsessively concerned our writers, all the way from *The Power of Sympathy,* whose appearance coincided with our birth as a nation, to *The Hamlet of A. MacLeish* or even Hyman Plutzik's Horatio poems."[28] Among the pantheon of American Hamlets, Fiedler cites Melville's Pierre Glendinning, Poe's Roderick Usher, "the Dimmesdale-Coverdale melancholics of Hawthorne," and Bellow's Herzog. For our purposes, however, the most suggestive figure he mentions is Faulkner's Quentin Compson.

Quentin's obsession with the disparity between the myth of the Old South and the reality of the New South (most evident in *Absalom, Absalom!*) and his more general love-hate relationship with his home region is simply a pathological exaggeration of what many young southern intellectuals felt during the cultural upheaval that began in the 1920s. The Agrarian movement, of which Warren was a part, consisted of sons of the Old South who saw their mother region repudiating past loyalties in favor of the whoredoms of industrialism. (All of their polemical efforts were directed toward upholding the honor of the old culture and convincing their motherland of the error of her ways.) Like Quentin Compson, Warren's Jack Burden is a neurotic young man who is caught in the middle of the South's cultural transformation. He comes from the dying aristocracy and is employed by a quintessential embodiment of the rising class—the redneck Willie Stark. (Although Warren never actually worked for Stark's model Huey Long, the Louisiana "Kingfish" did give him and Cleanth Brooks the money with which to start the *Southern Review*.) Still Jack's most deep-seated conflicts are generated less by the wider society than by the impact of that society on his own family situation.

In discussing *All the King's Men* as a modern tragedy, Heilman notes its "intra-family confrontations and injuries, the reprecussions on generation upon generation, as with Hamlet and Orestes" (p. 17). Similarly, it is within the matrix of family strife that Jack Burden has developed the personality which speaks to us in this novel. Like Hamlet, Jack is a brooding, philosophical young man who lacks a clear direction in life. His view of himself and of his world is communicated to us in interior monologues, the novelistic equivalent of the dramatic soliloquy. Among other things these monologues tell us that at the beginning of the novel Jack, like Hamlet, is a radical subjectivist who is blinded to any reality separate from his own perceptions and neuroses.

Although we do not have enough information about Hamlet's childhood to do more than speculate on the influences which shaped his personality, his ambivalent relationship with his parents seems to be of fundamental importance. Based on a much fuller depiction of Jack Burden's youth, we can say that a similar ambivalence lies at the heart of his malaise. As Louis D. Rubin, Jr. notes, Jack's decision to work for Willie is "an attempt to deny the sense of futility, of aimlessness, of unreality that he felt . . . as a child."[29]

The man whom Jack first knew as his father deserted the family when Jack was six. Although his mother brings a succession of new husbands into the house over the years, none of these men can replace Ellis Burden, the father whom Jack has lost. Instead, they simply become rivals for his mother's affection. Growing up in this environment, Jack looks upon his mother as a shallow and promiscuous woman who is incapable of true love.

It takes no great psychological insight to predict that Jack's upbringing will cause him serious difficulties in his later dealings with women. Although his youthful romance with Anne Stanton flounders primarily because of her disgust with his lack of purpose and vocation in life, that romance begins to fall apart with Jack's refusal to consummate his seduction of Anne. Later, his marriage to Lois fails at least in part because of his revulsion from her overt sensuality. Clearly, Jack's own sexual development has been warped by his attitude toward his mother.

The closest approximation of a truly erotic scene in *All the King's Men* probably is the one depicted in the following passage:

> She . . . took me by the sleeve of the forearm and drew me toward her. I didn't come at first. I just let her pull the arm. She didn't pull hard, but she kept on looking straight at me.
>
> I let myself go, and keeled over toward her. I lay on my back, with my head on her lap, the way I had known I would do. She let her left hand lie on my chest, the thumb and forefinger holding, and revolving back and forth, a button on my shirt, and her right hand on my forehead. . . . She had the trick of making a little island right in the middle of time. . . .
>
> Then she said, "You're tired, Son."[30]

When we analyze Hamlet's situation, we also find an unconventional mother-son relationship. At a conscious level, Hamlet's main grievance against Claudius is that the latter has murdered the elder Hamlet and has usurped his throne. As Ernest Jones and others have pointed out, however, the prince's anger seems to be aroused more genuinely by the marriage of Claudius and Gertrude. In the famous bedroom scene with his mother and elsewhere in the play, Hamlet dwells incessantly on the physical reality of Gertrude's copulation with her new husband. The tone here is less that of an aggrieved son than of a spurned lover.

Although the schizophrenic nature of Hamlet's courtship of Ophelia and his ultimate rejection of her love probably is the result of complex motivations, it is clear that his general view of women has been colored by his ambiguous feelings toward his mother. The misogynistic animus of his "get thee to a nunnery" speech is certainly not evoked by anything Ophelia has done. For Hamlet, she seems to exist as a mere pawn in the game he is playing with Gertrude. Indeed, when he lays his head in Ophelia's lap at the performance of *The Murder of Gonzago*, it is simply to taunt his mother. (Like Jack Burden, Hamlet has a thing about laps.)

In terms of the action of the play, however, Hamlet's more important parent is his father; for the revenge dilemma which bedevils Hamlet is caused by his father's death. Also, since he is bereft of his real father, he must create an ideal one out of his memory and his imagination. This ideal father appears to Hamlet—either in fact or in fancy—and places him under certain filial obligations. Thus, Hamlet is not searching for a father in the literal manner of a Telemachus, but is striving instead to establish—or reestablish—a bond with the past by doing his father's will. It is his misgivings about that task which create the central dramatic tension of the play.

Jack Burden's identity as a son is even more complex than Hamlet's, because Jack is dealing not with one father figure but with three. When the first of these fathers—Ellis Burden—deserts his family, Jack is plunged into the aimlessness and ennui of his formative and early adult years. This period in his life ends when Jack goes to work for Willie Stark. In signing on with Willie, who in effect becomes his surrogate-father, Jack is rejecting the past; for Willie is a man of the future, a Machiavellian upstart whose political movement is largely an insurgency against the oligarchy of the Old South from which Jack is fleeing. Jack's admiration for Willie is not unlike Hamlet's envy of Fortinbras.

His work on Willie's behalf ultimately leads to Jack's discovery of his true father. Told to dig up some dirt on Judge Irwin, Jack uncovers a scandal in the judge's past and confronts him with the incriminating evidence. Rather than submit to political blackmail, Irwin commits suicide. At this point Jack's mother reveals that Judge Irwin had been her son's real father. Like Hamlet, Jack has lost a father as a result of political intrigue; but, unlike Hamlet, he does not contemplate revenge.

An instructive contrast to Jack is provided by the character of Adam Stanton. Adam serves as a foil to Jack in much the same way as Laertes does to Hamlet. Adam is moved to seek vengeance against Willie Stark because Stark has "wronged" Adam's family: first, by apprising Adam—through Jack—of the late Governor Stanton's complicity in covering up Judge Irwin's scandal; and second, by taking Anne Stanton as his mistress. Similarly Laertes is moved to avenge *his* father and sister, both of whom are victims of Hamlet's madness. Eschewing rational deliberation, both Laertes and Adam Stanton instinctively seek violent retribution.

Jack Burden, however, transcends the pagan imperative of revenge and attains a more humanistic, even Christian, vision of the world. Although his arrival at this position is the result of many influences, it becomes complete when Jack is reunited with his original father figure, Ellis Burden—now a streetcorner evangelist. Unlike Hamlet, Jack Burden has found a father who is neither usurper nor pagan revenge god. Consequently, out of the materials of tragedy Warren has fashioned another, more affirmative type of Shakespearean drama—a comedy of forgiveness.

And yet, regardless of how much thematic parallels (and discontinuities) may tell us about *Hamlet* and *All the King's Men,* these are not sufficiently striking to make a case for direct influence. Nor does the available external evidence lead us very far. To my knowledge, the only Shakespeare play which Warren has ever mentioned in connection with his novel is *Julius Caesar.* Beyond that, we know only that he was reading Elizabethan tragedy at the time he was writing *All the King's Men.*[31] A couple of affinities in imagery and diction, however, raise the possibility that *Hamlet* was one of those tragedies.

To begin with, one of the most famous lines in *All the King's Men* is Willie Stark's articulation of the doctrine of Original Sin. "Man," he says, "is conceived in sin and born in corruption and he passeth from the stink of the didie to the stench of the shroud" (54). Although Willie's use of Elizabethan diction may suggest a Biblical influence, it is not difficult to imagine Hamlet's saying something very similar in the graveyard scene. As in "Love's Parable," Warren represents moral rot by evoking egregious images of physical decay.

In reading the interpolated Cass Mastern story,[32] one is also struck by certain Shakespearean parallels. When he contemplates suicide, for example, Cass ponders some of the same issues that plague Hamlet. Since Claudius has killed the elder Hamlet when the latter's soul was least prepared to be dispatched, the prince thinks it only right that Claudius be killed when circumstances would assure his damnation. Similarly, Cass feels that his own suicide and subsequent damnation would be the only fitting atonement for his betrayal of Duncan Trice. That he does not kill himself is attributed by Cass to the fact that "the Lord preserved me from self-slaughter" (p. 193). His word choice may even echo Hamlet's first soliloquy. Here, Shakespeare's protagonist laments the fact that the Everlasting has "fixed his canon 'gainst self-slaughter."

Perhaps more important than the evidence of specific passages, however, is the overall quality of Warren's language. As John M. Bradbury points out, "The 'rhetoric' of Warren's novels, particularly that of *All the King's Men,* has been harshly treated by several competent critics." Although rhetoric is a much-abused term, Bradbury contends that "it is the proper one for Warren if it be understood in its Elizabethan and baroque-metaphysical sense. In literary temperament Warren is much closer to sixteenth- and seventeenth-century ideals than to modern simplicity cults."[33]

Not only his rhetorical predilections but the very catholicity of his achievement suggests that Warren is indeed a throwback to another age. If the breadth of his intellect and the boldness of his imagination bespeak an Elizabethan sensibility, it is not surprising that his work has been influenced from time to time by that of the greatest Elizabethan. In a literal as well as a figurative sense, Robert Penn Warren is truly a Renaissance man.

NOTES

1. See *Robert Penn Warren Talking: Interviews 1950–1978,* ed. Floyd C. Watkins and John T. Hiers (New York: Random House, 1980), 267.

2. See Charles H. Bohner, *Robert Penn Warren* (New York: Twayne, 1964), 160.

3. Victor H. Strandberg makes essentially this same point in commenting on the entire body of Warren's criticism. See *The Poetic Vision of Robert Penn Warren* (Lexington: University Press of Kentucky, 1977), 34.

4. See Thomas Daniel Young, "A Little Divergence: The Critical Theories of John Crowe Ransom and Cleanth Brooks," in *The Possibilities of Order: Cleanth Brooks and His Work,* ed. Lewis P. Simpson (Baton Rouge: Louisiana State University Press, 1976), 171.

5. *Gentleman in a Dustcoat: A Biography of John Crowe Ransom* (Baton Rouge: Louisiana State University Press, 1976), 318.

6. From act 5, scene 2 of *Antony and Cleopatra.*

7. All quotations will be from the third edition (New York: Holt, Rinehart, and Winston, 1960).

8. In all fairness, it should be pointed out that Ransom did not deny Shakespeare's greatness as a dramatist. He simply argued that effective drama does not always make for good poetry. Brooks and Warren, however, do not see so sharp a distinction between the two genres.

9. Robert Penn Warren, *Selected Essays* (New York: Random House, 1958), 4–5.

10. Robert Penn Warren, *At Heaven's Gate* (New York: Harcourt, Brace, 1943), 194.

11. See L. Hugh Moore, Jr., *Robert Penn Warren and History (The Hague: Mouton, 1970), 38–39.*

12. In his introduction to the Modern Library edition of *All the King's Men,* Warren notes that all of the major characters in *At Heaven's Gate,* like those in the Seventh Circle of Dante's Hell, are violators of nature. See *Twentieth Century Interpretations of All the King's Men,* ed. Robert H. Chambers (Englewood Cliffs, New Jersey: Prentice Hall, 1977), 95.

13. See Louis D. Rubin, Jr., *The Wary Fugitives* (Baton Rouge: Louisiana State University Press, 1978), 357.

14. Robert Penn Warren, *Selected Poems 1923–1975* (New York: Random House, 1976), 284.

15. The allusion to Macbeth was pointed out to me by Victor H. Strandberg in personal correspondence dated December 7, 1980. I am indebted to Professor Strandberg for his insights concerning Shakespeare's influence on Warren's poetry.

16. John L. Stewart, *The Burden of Time: The Fugitives and Agrarians* (Princeton: Princeton University Press, 1965), 465–466.

17. In 1979 Warren published a "new version" of this poem. Although there is considerable difference in poetic technique between these two versions of *Brother to Dragons,* the poem's basic form and thematic concerns remain the same.

18. Robert Penn Warren, *Brother to Dragons* (New York: Random House, 1953), ix.

19. See Moore, 44.

20. The prominence of domestic tragedy in Shakespeare's history plays is discussed at great length in John Wilder's *The Lost Garden* (Totowa, New Jersey: Rowman, 1978).

21. Nevertheless, there have been numerous theatrical adaptations of Warren's verse dialogue, including "a 1955 dramatic reading for the BBC (which Warren had no part in), a staging at Harvard, a Broadway production canceled on opening day, reworkings in Seattle and at the American Place Theater in New York, and two productions directed by Adrian Hall in Providence in 1968 and 1973. (See Margaret Mills Harper, "Versions of History and *Brother to Dragons,*" in *Brother to Dragons: A Discussion,* ed. James A. Grimshaw, Jr. [Baton Rouge: Louisiana State University Press, 1983], 230). Finally, in 1976, Warren's text of *Brother to Dragons: A Play in Two Acts* appeared in the *Georgia Review.*

22. See "On the Underside of the Stone," *New York Times Book Review,* August 23, 1953, 8.

23. And yet, as Victor H. Strandberg has noted, the first three poems in *Promises* (1957) "adhere quite strictly to the stanza pattern of . . . the Shakespearean sonnet form." See *A Colder Fire* (Lexington: University of Kentucky Press, 1965), 280.

24. See Chambers, 93.

25. See Watkins and Hiers, 60. Elsewhere, Warren says of Huey Long: "The only time that his presence was ever felt in my classroom was when, in my Shakespeare course, I gave my little annual lecture on the political background of *Julius Caesar;* and then, for the two weeks we spent on the play, backs grew straighter, eyes grew brighter, notes were taken, and the girls stopped knitting in class, or repairing their faces." See *"All the*

King's Men The Matrix of Experience," in *Robert Penn Warren: A Collection of Essays,* ed. John L. Longley, Jr. (New York: New York University Press, 1965), 75.

26. See "Melpomene as Wallflower; or, the Reading of Tragedy," in Chambers, 23.

27. Arthur Mizener has noted "interesting similarities between *All the King's Men* and Shakespeare's 'dark' comedies, *Measure for Measure* and *Troilus and Cressida.*" See *Robert Penn Warren: A Collection of Critical Essays,* ed. Richard Gray (Englewood Cliffs, New Jersey: Prentice Hall, 1980), 54.

28. *The Collected Essays of Leslie Fiedler,* vol. 2 (New York: Stein and Day, 1971), 290. Warren himself has noted the appeal of the Hamlet story for another contemporary southern writer. See "A Note on the Hamlet of Thomas Wolfe" in Warren's *Selected Essays,* 170–183.

29. *Writers of the Modern South: The Faraway Country* (Seattle: University of Washington Press, 1963), 123.

30. *All the King's Men* (New York: Harcourt Brace, 1946), 119.

31. See Longley, 80.

32. This story, which is framed within a larger narrative and which sheds thematic light on that narrative, bears a relationship to the rest of *All the King's Men* not unlike that of *The Murder of Gonzaga* to the rest of *Hamlet.*

33. "Robert Penn Warren's Novels: The Symbolic and Textural Patterns," in Longley, 14.

Walker Percy's Lancelot:
The Shakespearean Threads

J. Madison Davis

Deriving their aesthetic theories from Alain Robbe-Grillet, Susan Sontag, and others, many contemporary authors eschew the use of allusion in an attempt to purify fiction of what they consider outdated appendages. James Joyce, say these writers, exploited the mythic in order to undermine the conventions of nineteenth-century prose, and now that postmodern writers are free of those conventions, they need to continue their "purification" of language by eliminating the traditional reliance on simile, metaphor, allusion, etc., so that they no longer write of what things are "like" but rather what they "are." Rhetorical devices are considered as antiquated as the works of George Pettie, John Lyly, and the other Elizabethan Euphuists. This aesthetic viewpoint owes much to Sartre, Camus, and the other existentialists who made it a moral imperative to avoid accepting the pre-existing conceptions of society (including literary conventions), and more stylistically to Hemingway than anyone would like to admit, even though nothing is thought more outmoded in some circles than Sartre's and Hemingway's constant grasping at "meaning," the bugaboo of many postmodernists.

Walker Percy addresses the problem of preconceptions in his essay "The Loss of the Creature" as he argues (along Sartrean lines) that it is nearly impossible for a modern person to experience the Grand Canyon directly:

> The thing is no longer the thing as it confronted the Spaniard; it is rather that which has already been formulated—by picture postcard, geography book, tourist folders, and the words *Grand Canyon*. As a result of this preformulation, the source of the sightseer's pleasure undergoes a shift. . . . The highest point, the term of the sightseer's satisfaction, is not the sovereign discovery of the thing before him; it is rather the measuring up of the thing to the criterion of the preformed symbolic complex.[1]

He goes on to argue that the modern world, with its communications, education, and civic helpfulness, has destroyed contemporary man's ability to experience anything directly and that only the catastrophic (a heart attack victim may really *see* his hand for the first time), or a constant struggle against the "packaging" of the world can give humanity the ability to experience the world for what it is, to look "with a wild surmise" from a peak in Darien.

One would therefore assume from the essay that Percy, too, avoids allusion and metaphor as standing between the reader and the direct experience of the writing. Upon reading his works, however, one discovers that far from avoiding these literary devices Percy revels in them. With a pronounced Christian orientation, an existentialist's concern with the future of humanity, and profound regret for what mankind seems to be doing to itself, Percy appears to be writing in direct opposition to his essay, and certainly in contrast to much postmodernist aesthetics. Percy liberally interweaves references to an extraordinary variety of major and minor literary and philosophical figures throughout his novels. Page after page we encounter scholastic philosophers, popular writers, and literary titans. He even dares name the main character in *Love Among the Ruins* Dr. Thomas More. Yet *Time*'s reviewer, in praising *The Moviegoer,* wrote that Percy "has a rare talent for making his people look and sound as though they were being seen and heard for the first time by anyone."[2] How can he accomplish this freshness with such traditional devices?

A complete analysis of literary allusions in Percy would take at least a book, but an examination of specific Shakespearean allusions in *Lancelot,* the 1977 award-winning novel often considered his most successful work, reveals more than just the obvious influence of the playwright upon the novelist, but also helps explain the seeming contradiction in his intentional, heavy use of allusion and his aesthetic and philosophical comments. Certainly, one of the most complex tapestries he weaves is *Lancelot.* The narrator, Lancelot Andrewes Lamar, is an upper-class southern lawyer who has been confined to a mental hospital because of the commission of some crime. He is telling his story to a priest, Father John, who has been his friend since boyhood, although they have been separated for a while. There is a woman in the next cell who is recovering from the traumatic effects of a brutal gang rape and with whom Lance is trying to communicate by tapping, in the same way that prisoners of war communicated. As the novel progresses, the reader discovers that Lance blew up his antebellum mansion with himself, his wife, and the murdered body of her adulterous lover inside. The novel is interesting enough on the simple level of plot, despite the confessional device (a convention all too familiar from novels like Gide's *The Immoralist* and Camus' *The Fall*).[3] Yet *Lancelot* is much more than an interesting plot. It peels like an onion, layer upon layer.

The most obvious allusion is to the Arthurian legends of Lancelot du Lac, and many critics have commented upon these thematic relations. Lance calls himself "Lancelot" and his friend "Percival" (or "Parsifal") on numerous occasions throughout the book. Lancelot du Lac and Percival were the only two knights of the Round Table to see the Holy Grail and Lance and Father John are thus implied to have seen something no one else has seen, although Lance remarks, "I Lancelot and you Percival. The only two to see the Grail if you recall. Did you find the Grail? You don't look like it" (176–77).[4] This makes it unclear whether Father John has found that for which he was looking. As Robert Coles points out, exactly what constitutes the Holy Grail in Percy's novel "is as hard to grasp or describe as the legendary one of the Age of Chivalry."[5]

Coles also notes the relationship between Lancelot Lamar, Sir Lancelot and *The Divine Comedy*. *Lancelot* significantly begins with an epigraph from *Purgatorio:* "He sank so low that all means/ for his salvation were gone/ except showing him the lost people/ for this I visited the region of the dead. . . ." Dante at this point is being rebuked by a vision of Beatrice. He has been unable to face the reality of his own moral failings. Lance, too, has not been able "to look candidly into his own heart," "to figure out how to live a life." Dante's vision of Beatrice and Lancelot's of the Grail both point up the defects of these heroes, just as the memory of infidelity and horror reveal the failures of

Lance's life. The point then becomes what the hero will do about this self-discovery. Instead of becoming obsessed with the past, he must dispose of it, forget it, and live in a way that reflects his new vision.[6]

Coles further discusses the relations between *Lancelot* and *Idylls of the King,* but Tennyson merely begins the list of literary and philosophical writers used in direct and indirect ways to compose this multilayered novel. Critics have noted the reference in Lance's name to sermonist Lancelot Andrewes of the Renaissance, who contributed to the King James translation of the Bible and to the philosophic foundations of the Church of England. Lewis A. Lawson notes allusions to *Huckleberry Finn, A Farewell to Arms, The Prisoner of Chillon, La Dame aux camélias,* and discusses the Sartrean elements of Lance's psychology.[7] Also significant is Lance's reading of Raymond Chandler, who created Philip Marlowe, a modern-day knight in quest of truth in a seedy, corrupted Los Angeles (in one novel, Marlowe even searches for a woman with the surname Grail). The resemblances between Marlowe's quests and Lance's search for truth in a corrupted world are many.

Critics, however, have only barely touched upon the Shakespearean allusions, which occur frequently and contribute much to the complexity and beauty of Percy's tapestry.[8] They have not been carefully examined previously, because they are clearly secondary to the more obvious allusions. Furthermore, it is virtually impossible to be a writer in the twentieth century and not be influenced in a host of direct and indirect ways by Shakespeare's plays. Therefore it would not be particularly significant that a writer like Percy should refer to a variety of Shakespeare's lines and characters, often without a clear understanding of what is implied by a quotation or often with only the most stereotyped notion of what a casually mentioned character like Romeo, Falstaff, or Caliban is all about. A reader is willing to accept such offhand allusions for what they are—conventions, of exactly the sort that contemporary writers like the Modernists (and before them, the Romantics) have attempted to avoid.

None of Percy's writings, however, can be said to be either "casual" or "offhand," and his method of weaving Shakespearean threads throughout reveals a great deal about his intention as a novelist. Percy plainly feels he has a mission. He is intent upon saying something significant about the world as it exists. His writing exhibits consummate craftsmanship, each part fitting snugly into the whole (occasionally to the degree that some of his work drifts dangerously toward predictability), and if an allusion is made to a Shakespearean work, it is obviously to a significant purpose. Walker Percy is not dropping names when a reference to a Shakespearean character recurs several times throughout *Lancelot,* any more than he is being casual in using the legends of Lancelot du Lac, Percival, Sir Turquine, and Merlin.

The first allusion to a Shakespearean character that reappears throughout *Lancelot* is at the beginning of the second chapter. Lance has invited Father John back for a second visit, during which he has promised to try to remember the past and explain the events leading up to his incarceration.

> We [Lance and Father John] knew each other by several names depending on the oblique and obscure circumstances of our lives— and our readings. I bet I remember your names better than you. To begin with, you were simply Harry, when you lived at Northumberland close to us on the River Road and we went to school together. Later you were known variously as Harry Hotspur, a misnomer because though you were pugnacious you were not much of a fighter. Also as Prince Hal, because you seemed happy only in whorehouses. Also as Northumberland, after the house you lived in. Also as Percival and Parsifal, who found the Grail and brought life to a dead land (pp. 9–10).

Most of the references, of course, are to *The First Part of King Henry IV,* a play which seems to have affected Percy significantly as some references to it also appear in *The Moviegoer,* his first novel. From the beginning of *Henry IV, Part I,* a conflict is set up between the proud, bellicose Hotspur (whose father is Earl of Northumberland and whose surname is Percy), and the apparently dissolute heir to the throne, Prince Hal. At the beginning, Hotspur appears to be the logical hero of the play; he has all the noble qualities. Even Hal's father broods:

Yea, there thou mak'st me sad and mak'st me sin
In envy that my Lord Northumberland
Should be the father to so blest a son—
A son who is the theme of honor's tongue,
Amongst a grove the very straightest plant,
Who is sweet Fortune's minion and her pride,
Whilst I, looking on the praise of him,
See riot and dishonor stain the brow
Of my young Harry. O that it could be proved
That some night-tripping fairy had exchang'd
In cradle-clothes our children where they lay,
And call'd mine Percy, his Plantagenet!
                          (*Henry IV, Part 1*, 1.1.78–79[9])

Although Shakespeare plants the seeds of Hotspur's weakness
(his overriding pride) in the next few lines, this is easily over-
looked in the first appearance of Prince Hal, joking with Falstaff
in act 1, scene 2 and agreeing to be the "madcap" and go along
with a robbery. One's sympathies are completely with the
careworn king who would trade a Plantagenet for a Percy.
Shakespeare, however, adds yet another ingredient to the conflict as Hal ends the scene:

Yet herein will I imitate the sun,
Who doth permit the base contagious clouds
To smother up his beauty from the world,
That when he please again to be himself,
Being wanted, he may be more wond'red at
By breaking through the foul and ugly mists
Of vapors that did seem to strangle him.
                          (*Henry IV, Part I*, 197–203).

The seeds of the entire drama are planted in these two scenes.
As Hotspur's pride becomes arrogance, as his warrior's self-
confidence is exposed as choler and swagger, he reveals his true
nature and the king's wish to replace his son seems foolish. Hal,
on the other hand, also reveals the truth of his nature. By the
end, he is everything a young Prince of Wales should be, show-

ing generosity to a courageous foe and being welcomed to his father's side to fight Glendower and the Earl of March. The execution of this simple reversal is one of Shakespeare's greatest achievements, and although it is a complex play psychologically *Henry IV* has the simple resonance of mythology, the echoes of a story that evokes as much in the listeners as it reveals about the characters.

Walker Percy, of course, exploits this mythological tone, returning several times to references to Hal and Hotspur. Lance and Father John have found different ways of living. Lance found it necessary to go through the commission of murder and arson to be reawakened. He has lived his life solipsistically, refusing to face the realities of the modern world. He has deceived himself, for example, as a liberal civil rights lawyer helping to free blacks from generations of slavery and servitude, yet maintaining his squire-like relation to them. Were Lance's counterpart Hotspur also not so wrapped up in himself—and in his father's ambitions (note that Lance's father was a dreamy believer in the aristocratic tradition of the Old South)—he could have risen to a position of power in Henry's court, a position possibly surpassing the Prince's.

Father John was nicknamed Harry Hotspur, but he is told by Lance that it was a misnomer and that Prince Hal is his appropriate nickname, because he was happy only in whorehouses. The comparison goes further than that. In their youth, it was Lancelot who was the success. He ran a football 110 yards against Alabama and then became bored because the Lamars "lived for great deeds" (p. 58). He became a liberal lawyer in the heroic struggle of the 1960s and arrogantly enjoyed being disliked. By the 1970s, however, blacks and whites had turned against liberals. "In the end, liberals become a pain in the ass, even to themselves" (p. 59). Lancelot's career, like Hotspur's, starts as heroic and then steadily declines. Father John, on the other hand, "imitates the sun." His nature is concealed. There was not the slightest indication (at least to Lance) that he had any religious feelings whatsoever when they were boys. He went off to the seminary "out of a clear sky . . . the ultimate reckless lifetime thing." He went from "unbeliever to priest, leapfrogging on the

way some eight hundred million ordinary Catholics" (p. 61).
Even then, it wasn't sufficient to be an ordinary New Orleans
priest; he became a missionary in Africa.

One might also make a great deal of the name "Percy," as in
"Henry Percy" (Hotspur) and thereby imagine the narrator to be
the persona of the author.[10] Others, noting that "Percy" is the
diminutive of "Percival," locate the persona in Father John. Obviously, the author is simultaneously one and the other and both:
Walker Percy created them and therefore is all of them. Furthermore, one of Lancelot's problems with the modern world is its
lack of heroism. He cannot find the great deeds which would
separate the Hotspurs from the Hals, the Falstaffs from the
Douglasses, the Lancelots from the Sir Turquines. "Notice the
poster near the old colored entrance of the movie," says Lance
ruefully. "It's new. *Deep Throat* where once we saw *Henry V*
and *Key Largo*" (p. 255). Though Father John seems to have
done the nobler thing with his life, why is it that Lance keeps
indicating that John is unhappy, dissatisfied, by implication unsure that his efforts have had meaning? Lance's voyage of self-
discovery has clarified some things, but made others more bewil-
dering, and in this vein makes the allusions to *King Lear* clearer.

References to *King Lear* appear several times in the book and
the parallels to Lance's story are quite plain. Both *Lear* and
Henry IV are plays of self-discovery. Hal discovers himself in his
proper role as future king. Lear discovers the foolishness and
weakness of his human nature. As Judah Stampfer remarked of
Lear,

Lear, at the beginning of the play, embodies all that man looks for-
ward to in a world in which, ultimately, nothing is secure. . . . Thus,
. . . Lear activates the latent anxiety at the core of the human
condition, the fear not only of unexpected catastrophe but that even
what seems like success may be a delusion, masking corruption,
crime, and almost consummated failure. . . . By the time he enters
prison, he has paid every price and been stripped of everything a
man can lose, even his sanity, in payment for folly and pride. . . .
And with Lear's death, each audience . . . shares and releases the
most private and constricting fear to which mankind is subject, the

fear . . . that the covenant, once broken, can never be established
. . . the fear, in other words, that we inhabit an imbecile universe.[12]

Stampfer could nearly be describing Lancelot, and his story can
be interpreted as tragedy. Its hero begins possessing nearly
everything for which a man could wish. He is the scion of an
"old" family, he has a beautiful wife and children, a good home,
a peaceful life, and a respected role in the community, although
he seems to have allowed too much inertia into his marriage,
probably because of his drinking. Yet nothing is secure. Belle
Isle, the "beautiful isle," like Lear's Britain, is doomed. Chance
(or fate, or the gods) intervenes. His eyes are opened by the
discovery that his daughter Siobhan's blood type is "O," an
impossibility given Lance and his wife Margot's blood types.
Siobhan is illegitimate and the probable father, Robert Merlin, is
directing a movie at Belle Isle. The "O" becomes zero, becomes
nothing, and as Lear says, "Nothing will come of nothing!"

The universe cracks open for Lance just as it cracks open for
Lear. Lance's self-deceptions are destroyed. He must know the
truth and engages in an elaborate surveillance scheme to find out
exactly how he fits into Margot's and the moviemakers' lives.
Like Oedipus, he must uncover the pollution. "I knew only that
it was necessary to know, to know only as the eyes know"
(p. 236). Like Lear, he creates the subsequent disasters by opening the door to darkness. In the end, like Lear, he is surrounded
by bloodshed and is raging in madness. In a way, Lancelot is an
even more tragic figure because he has been spared death. He
must go on living in an imbecile universe, and, depending on
one's view of his final words, is deceiving himself once again in
the belief that he can create a "Third Revolution" that will restore the world to sanity, and is thereby creating the circumstances for even more disaster. The universe, as Lear and
Oedipus discover, will not cooperate with our fantasies. Lancelot has merely adopted a new set of illusions.

Lance, like Lear, has three "daughters." Lucy has betrayed
him by becoming involved in a bisexual relationship with actors
Troy Dana and Raine Robinette. His son betrays him by moving
to New Orleans and going gay. In Lance's view of the boy he

can, without much difficulty, be thought of as a second "daughter"; Lance always emphasizes his femininity. His youngest daughter, Siobhan, plays a Cordelia-like role. Her "O," her "nothing," leads Lance on his quest for knowledge. Like Cordelia for Lear, Siobhan has in no way truly betrayed Lance. She has, in one moment of discovery, been removed as his actual daughter; yet she remains the best of his children. Even if one eliminates the son from consideration as a "daughter," one might argue that Margot, who is much younger than Lance and uses her body and his sexual vanity to get control of his house, is much like Regan and Goneril who use their easy speeches of love and Lear's vanity to seize his kingdom. "The simple and amazing truth," says Lance, "is that when she finished fixing up Belle Isle, she also somehow finished with me" (p. 120). Later he reflects, "The truth is, it never crossed my mind in my entire sweet southern life that there was such a thing as a lustful woman. Another infinite imponderable. Infinitely appalling. What hath God wrought?" (p. 129).

Furthermore, the novel builds up to the hurricane in which the climax occurs, just as the play builds up to the storm. The movie, which Merlin, Jacoby, and the others are making, also climaxes in a storm. In its final scene the planter's daughter (played by Margot) and the "Christ-like hippie stranger" (played by Dana) come to rescue the planter (Merlin) from an oncoming hurricane. The planter, however, welcomes the apocalyptic fury and his daughter leaves with the stranger: "After the farewell, the planter, who is not so much prejudiced as indifferent, caught up by aesthetic rather than social concerns, returns to the house alone." (p. 197). The movie thus mirrors the events of the novel, just as the novel (and the movie) reflect Shakespeare's play. Merlin is standing in Lance's place as the lord of Belle Isle, just as he has usurped his fatherhood. Perhaps because of this, Lance sees himself in a special relationship with Merlin. He recognizes in Merlin his own world-weariness and spares him from the carnage to go "back to Africa to find his youth. To see leopard" (p. 201). Merlin is in a spiritual crisis similar to Lance's.

Prophetically, in shooting the last scene of the movie, Jacoby says to Merlin, " 'I want more of a Lear-like effect, Bob. . . . You know, mad king raging on the heath, wild-eyed, hair blowing' " (p. 197). When the storm does arrive Lance's internal struggle expresses itself in violence, as if to mimic the violence of the hurricane. Like Lear in the storm, Lance is reduced to madness. He fills the house with methane from an abandoned oil well, and slaughters Jacoby with Margot looking on from the adulterous bed. Finally he has seen the truth, and like Lear the seeing has cost him everything. In the moment when the house explodes, Lancelot believes he has discovered himself: "I was wheeling slowly up into the night like Lucifer blown out of hell, great wings spread against the starlight. *I knew everything*" (p. 246, emphasis added).

The layers of allusion, then, are many and dense, and a close examination of any of the carefully chosen allusions— Shakespearean and otherwise—reveals their importance in accomplishing Percy's objective: to make the reader examine the meaning and implications of life in contemporary society. "Every explorer names his island Formosa, beautiful" writes Percy in "The Loss of the Creature"[13] and Lance Lamar of Belle Isle is such an explorer. He is a searcher like Lancelot, like Dante, like Philip Marlowe, like Lear—like the protagonists in all of Percy's novels.[14] In his own mind he is a hero obsessed with seeing the truth, the "Unholy Grail," the alternative to a decaying society. What he insists on knowing is vouchsafed to no one, and the quest for it is in itself a kind of faithless arrogance: humanity is not meant to understand the ways of God. One might ask, if Percy's intention is to have us experience Lance's story as directly as possible, why does he remove the reader's sovereignty by imposing the figures of Lear, Hal, Philip Marlowe, Lancelot du Lac, Lucifer, and others, upon the main character? Why not simply present him as he "is"? Why is the story multilayered with what many contemporary critics would call antiquated literary devices?

This question, of course, misses the point. Percy is actually quite an "old-fashioned" novelist by the standards of amoral, meaninglessness-is-meaning postmodernists. He makes it clear that he considers himself a Christian novelist. He has also been

heavily influenced by the existentialists. Though he considers
the atheistic existentialists, such as Sartre, to have gone wrong,
even that aspect of existentialism requires that a human being
create essence by action. Therefore, a moral purpose is required. Percy's intention is obviously to have his novel make its
readers consider the nature of life in contemporary society. The
readers' sovereignty is actually increased by forcing them to
deal with the many directions in which all these allusions simultaneously lead. He is forcing existential choice on his readers.
Although his books vent much spleen about the corruption and
decadence of contemporary existence, Percy rarely makes any
overt recommendations about how we ought to be living. Even
when he does, the advice may come from a madman like Lance
Lamar. As Jerome Christensen argues, Lance's monologue col-
lapses under the weight of its own message, but its collapse *is* its
message.[15] Afterwards, it is up to the reader to act. Percy's message is never a direct exhortation: "You should be doing this or
that."

Interpreting his works as if they had a simple message is therefore a mistake. Percy makes no pretense of having seen either
the Holy or the "Unholy" Grail. The mysteries of the universe
are still a mystery to him. His novels are designed to reveal the
complexity of the human condition: the mixed emotions, the
reconciling of our concept of ourselves with our reality and of
our concept of the external world with our preconceptions—the
problem of how we should live in the world. Part of that complexity is the layering of past on present. Lear becomes all old
men; Hotspur becomes all passionate, proud young men. By
metaphor, anyone can become a Lear or a Hal or a Hotspur, and
although in the final analysis no one can be anything other than
an imitation of these (like Lance Lamar), one lives much of
one's life attempting to impose the outlines of various fictional
characters or fictionalized human beings on one's own behavior.

Percy is not just using the Shakespearean (and other) conventions to exploit the mythologic resonances that emerge from
them. He is showing us a character and a society tangled in a
web of mythologies. Lance is enmeshed as much in Jeff Davis,
Rhett Butler, Sterling Hayden, and his own father as he is in the

Shakespearean figures. His character is partly derived from them, and his problem, like ours, is the inability to see beyond given concepts. When Lance finally frees himself to believe in a new world in a "pure" land, Virginia, isn't he really turning his personal sovereignty over to the American mythologic vision of the New Jerusalem? One expects that Lance's new life will end no better than his last. Our symbols *are* our reality. As Percy concludes in his essay, "The Mystery of Language":

> The existentialists have taught us that what man is cannot be grasped by the sciences of man. . . . Man is not merely a higher organism responding to and controlling his environment. He is, in Heidegger's words, that being in the world whose calling is to find a name for Being, to give testimony to it, and to provide for it a clearing.[16]

NOTES

1. Walker Percy, "The Loss of the Creature," in *The Message in the Bottle* (New York: Farrar, Straus, and Giroux, 1975), 47.

2. Rev. *The Moviegoer. Time,* 19 May 1961, 105.

3. Deborah J. Barrett, "Discourse and Intercourse: The Conversion of the Priest in Percy's *Lancelot,*" *Critique* 23 (1981–82): 5.

4. This and all subsequent page numbers in parentheses refer to Walker Percy, *Lancelot* (New York: Farrar, Straus, and Giroux, 1977).

5. Robert Coles, *Walker Percy: An American Search* (Boston: Little, Brown, 1978), 218.

6. Coles, 217–221.

7. Lewis A. Lawson, "The Fall of the House of Lamar," in *The Art of Walker Percy,* ed. Panthea Reid Broughton. (Baton Rouge: Louisiana State Univ. Press, 1979), 219–244.

8. Lewis A. Lawson mentions it only briefly in "Walker Percy's Silent Character," *Mississippi Quarterly* 33 (Spring 1980): 128.

9. This and all subsequent quotations from Shakespeare are from *The Riverside Shakespeare,* G. Blakemore Evans, textual ed. (Boston: Houghton Mifflin, 1974), and follow the line numbering of this edition.

10. Lancelot's voice is so powerful that too many have assumed that Percy speaks through him as William James O'Brien points out in "Walker Percy's *Lancelot:* A Beatrician Visit to the Region of the Dead," *Southern Humanities Review* 15 (1981): 153.

11. Barrett, 10–11.

12. "The Catharsis of *King Lear,*" in *Shakespeare: Modern Essays in Criticism,* ed. Leonard F. Dean (New York: Oxford Univ. Press, 1967), 374–375.

13. Percy, "The Loss of the Creature," 46.

14. Tracy Lischer, "Walker Percy's Cerberus: Love, Sexuality, and Sin," *Christianity and Literature,* 30 (1981): 34.

15. Jerome Christensen, "*Lancelot:* Sign for the Times," in *Walker Percy: Art and Ethics,* ed. Jac Tharpe (Jackson: Univ. Press of Mississippi, 1980), 119.

16. Percy, "The Mystery of Language," in *The Message in the Bottle,* 158.